How To Podcast

Four Simple Steps To Broadcast Your Message To
The Entire Connected Planet ... Even If You Don't
Know What Podcasting Really Is

Paul Colligan

http://HowToPodcastBook.com
http://HowToPodcastApp.com
http://HowToPodcastTraining.com

About Paul Colligan

Paul Colligan is passionate about helping others leverage technology to grow their businesses. His goal is to expand your reach and revenue, with reduced stress and no drama. His lifestyle and business strategies are designed to tackle the challenges and opportunities of today's ever-changing information economy.

Paul has played a key role in the launch of dozens of successful internet products that have garnered tens of millions of visitors in traffic and revenue. He's been the secret weapon behind dozens of best-selling authors on Amazon, number one podcasts on Itunes, and millions of views on YouTube. Previous projects have included work with StoryBrand, The U.S. State Department, Traffic Geyser, Rubicon International, Piranha Marketing, Microsoft, Pearson Education and more.

He is also a popular speaker on technology topics and has presented at events around the world including BlogWorld and New Media Expo, The European Business Podcasting Summit, Google Tech Talks, MacWorld, Social Media Success Summit, Inbound Marketing Summit, Social Media Marketing World and Microsoft TechEd. Paul is the CEO of the Podcast Partnership, creator of The Podcast Industry Report and has authored eleven books including current Amazon bestsellers *How To Stream Video 2016*, *How to Podcast 2016* and *YouTube Strategies 2016*.

Paul lives in Portland, Oregon with his wife and daughters and enjoys theater, music, great food and travel. If you are interested in his latest projects and his thoughts on the world of new media, visit http://PaulColligan.com.

About The Podcast Partnership

The Podcast Partnership was established in 2006 to provide the leadership, tools and best practices needed for people seeking to do *real business* with their Podcast. Check out http://PodcastPartnership.com for more information.

PODCASTPARTNERSHIP

NEED	OPTION
Learn how to Podcast	**How To Podcast Program** Learn the four simple steps to create your podcast and broadcast your message to the planet. OR Learn Paul's proven method to create your podcast and broadcast your message to the planet in four simple steps. **HowToPodcastBook.com** **HowToPodcastCourse.com**
Simple podcasting system	**Dial Talk Done** Producing a podcast can be as easy as making a phone call using this automated system. **DialTalkDone.com**
Podcast consulting, production, and management	**The Podcast Partnership** Personalized consulting and full podcast production service available to a select group of clients. **PodcastPartnership.com**

Table of Contents

About This Book

My name is Paul Colligan, and I've been in podcasting pretty much since day one. I love podcasting and training others on how to succeed with it. My wonderful clients at The Podcast Partnership are leading the way in doing real business with their podcasts and I'm thrilled to be a part of their success.

This isn't my first book on podcasting. I have two other popular books about podcasting in print: *The Business Podcasting Bible* (released in 2006) and *Podcast Strategies* (released in 2012 to a number one ranking in seven different countries). I still love both of these books and all that they represent, but they basically assume that you already know what podcasting is, and that you want to do more with it. This new book is a revised and updated version of *How To Podcast 2016*, and is geared toward an audience who is completely new to podcasting.

Why another book? In the last ten years, as podcasting has gained momentum, I began to notice one thing - people just keep making podcasting more difficult than it needed to be. As a result, we're more than a decade into this space, and some people still aren't podcasting because they think it's too complicated. I'd like to change that.

I hate unnecessary complication. You only have so many hours in the day, and you don't need to waste them trying to sift through someone's 200-page technical explanation of a simple process. Or worse, find yourself watching a 20-part video series or wading through a weekend-long boot camp. You need to get back to what you do well - running your business. Podcasting doesn't have to be complicated, and I'm here to show you how it's done.

Previous editions of this book were dated: "How To Podcast 2015, "How To Podcast 2016," etc. From this point on I'm going to keep it a single title that only changes volume numbers. Want to know about any major changes in the podcasting space since your purchase of this version? Make sure to register your copy of the book at http://HowToPodcastBook.com and you'll be updated automatically.

Is this book the whole story on podcasting? No. As the title states, this is a book on *How To Podcast* and I'll show you how in four simple steps.

Note: This is NOT a technical book for Nerds!

This book is for regular individuals and business owners who want to understand podcasting so they can get their message out there, simply, quickly, and effectively. When it comes down to it, podcasting is about the content, not technology. If you're a sound or video professional looking for a highly technical book, please put this one down.

This is also not a *How to Make Money in Podcasting* or a *How to Market Your Podcast* book. Instead it is, quite simply, *How To Podcast*, in four simple steps. Of course, you're free to go on to any of those other topics once you're done with this short book.

This book is the exact process we use to produce podcasts at The Podcast Partnership.

It's four steps .... really. That's it.

And this book explains them all.

Thanks for picking it up.

Register This Book About The Redirect Links

Please take a moment now and register this book at the link below. By registering this book, I'll be able to keep you up to date by email on any major changes that you need to know about. If I make a change to the book, I'll make sure you have a digital copy. Registration will also get you access to the bonus membership site I described earlier.

Again, to register this book, visit http://HowToPodcastBook.com My promise to you is that I'll keep this book updated for the entire year. Register the book and you'll find out when the next updated version is released. I'll make sure you get that at a ridiculously good rate, too.

The Videos And The Bonuses

I reference a number of videos in this book that are yours for having purchased this book. Just follow the links to watch - or click on them directly if you are reading a digital version.

Check out the *Bonuses* chapter for special deals and extra's just for registering the book.

Wow, This Book is Short!

Yes, I purposely kept this book short so that you could finish it quickly and get to work. I don't want you debating platforms or microphone types. I want you broadcasting your message to the world.

Here's the thing: your first podcast will be your worst podcast, and the sooner you get that one recorded and published, the sooner you'll get better at it. Once that happens, it might be time to look at elements which are a bit more complicated, but between now and then, let's get your first podcast LIVE.

Paul, I Found A Typo — Or A Mistake — Or, You're Grammar Weren't Good!

I bet you did. Typos are going to happen. It's actually one of the reasons I prefer podcasting over book authoring — nobody knows when I'm spelling things wrong in front of a microphone!

If you find something that needs a fix, point it out on the Facebook page (or email) mentioned below and I just might give you a shout-out for your awesome grammarizing (yeah, that's a word) in the next release of this book.

Affiliate Disclaimer

I create commercial content that helps pay the bills. I am what many call an information marketer. Often, I am the provider and owner of the products and services that I recommend.

Occasionally, the companies that provide the products and services I recommend compensate me. It is sometimes direct, sometimes indirect — but it is there.

If this concerns you, no problem. Return this book. We can still be friends.

At all times, I only recommend products I use (or would tell my Mom to use.) You have my promise there.

Let's Continue the Conversation

The internet continues to change on a regular basis, and I can pretty much promise you that once we send this book to be published, many of these changes will have already kicked in. The best way to stay informed on the changes that impact you is to register your book at http://HowToPodcastBook.com.

We also set up a Facebook page specifically for this book at http://www.Facebook.com/HowToPodcast. When you launch your podcast as a result of this book, make sure you post it there, too. You deserve the attention and acclaim that we'll be sending your way when you do.

My blog is online at http://www.PaulColligan.com — drop by and say hi!

In terms of social networking, you can find me in all the usual places:

http://PaulColligan.com/Twitter

http://PaulColligan.com/Facebook

http://PaulColligan.com/Instagram

http://PaulColligan.com/YouTube

Let's get out there and podcast!

Paul Colligan

HowToPodcastBook@Gmail.com

Portland, Oregon

June 2017

What Is Podcasting?

Podcasting is, quite simply:

Audio or video made available online for easy on-demand consumption and/or subscription-based delivery.

That's it.

You were expecting more, weren't you? Others have certainly tried to make it out to be more than that. Of course, there are details and nuances, but that's podcasting in a nutshell.

Yes, it is simple — but there is power in simplicity.

That's it. The whole Apple, iTunes, iPad, iPhone, Apple TV podcasting thing — it's all possible because of the fact that it's *audio or video made available online for easy on-demand consumption and/or subscription-based delivery.*

Apple recently announced 10 billion podcast streams in 2016. This is a media format that has reached mainstream.

But it's not just an Apple thing. What about the podcasts on a Google device, a Microsoft phone, a connected car stereo, or some other platform out there that supports podcasts? Those too are just simply *audio or video made available online for both easy on-demand consumption and/or subscription-based delivery.*

One single podcast will work on any device that can access your content. You don't need to make things specifically for an iPad, Android device, connected car stereo, or any other device or platform. Once your podcast is up and running, it works on any device for anyone. In that way, it is just like radio or television. It makes no difference if the listener gets your content on a Sony or a Hitachi device. What really matters, in fact, is that they *can* get your content.

Why do others make it so complicated?

There are a number of theories as to why some have tried to make podcasting more complicated than it needs to be. They range from the conspiracy level, *"they can't charge you as much once you realize how easy it is"* — to the more human explanation, *"some people are so excited by the tech that they want to share every single element of it with you, even if you don't need it."*

When I was first putting this book together, I posted this definition online to a few podcaster sites to see what they thought. If someone had a simpler way of explaining the process, I certainly wanted to share it with you. No one did.

We'll never really know why some people like to make things complicated, and it doesn't matter anyway. This book is about making it simple so that in the end, you can get your podcast up and running quickly.

I'll say it one more time — podcasting is, simply: *audio or video made available online for easy on-demand consumption and/or subscription-based delivery.*

Let's break down our definition and look at it with a bit more focus and clarity.

Audio or Video ...

Almost all audio or video media is digital now, and conversion is easy for the few pieces that aren't yet digitized. The important benefit of digital media is that it's stored on a hard drive or a chip somewhere — not in a warehouse or on store shelves with a distinct physical copy for each and every person. The same scale that quickly made Apple the biggest retailer of music is now the force behind *your* message. How cool is that?

As technology has advanced, digital media has improved as well. This means that the files are getting smaller and smaller in size, making them easier to send over the internet. The quality is getting higher and higher, meaning they look and sound better. Oh, the joys of technology!

....Made Available Online....

Because your media is placed online, it's accessible to anyone with a connection to the internet. Because the internet is everywhere, accessing your content isn't a question of "Apple vs. Windows" or "iPhone vs. Android" — it's available anytime, anywhere, to anyone who knows where to find it.

....For Easy On-Demand Consumption....

Making your content easily accessible is incredibly simple to do with the existing podcasting and web infrastructure. The great part is that you pay NO licensing fees to make your media available to the world, and everything that you're going to need in order to achieve that global exposure — at minimal cost — is included in this book.

Okay, so there are no licensing fees for podcasting, but what does it cost to make your audio and video available to the world? There are ways to distribute this easily-accessible content to the world for less than the price of a large pizza each month. We'll discuss that in more depth in Step Two. You might notice in our bonus section that one of the biggest names in podcasting is going to give you your first month for free, just for picking up this book.

....And/or Subscription-Based Delivery.

Finally, your content needs a subscription option, so that when someone finds out they really like your message, they can subscribe. This feature alone remains one of the biggest strengths of podcasting. With subscription-based delivery, every time you release a new episode, your subscribers will get it automatically, 100% spam-free. This is not just an iPhone or Smart TV feature, nor is it owned by Apple. This is, quite simply, the backbone of podcasting and you can set it up very quickly.

Not everyone uses the subscription element of podcasting, and that's unfortunate. Once someone has found content they like from a source they trust, it is imperative to make sure they understand that they can get new episodes automatically, usually with just the click of a button.

Is That It?

Is that everything? Can it really be so simple?

Yes. What's more, this book will cover EVERYTHING you need to get your podcast up and running. We'll even explain it to you in just four simple steps.

If you're looking for something more complicated, you're not going to find it here. I hope that's okay.

Let's get to it!

STEP 1
CREATE DIGITAL MEDIA

STEP 2
PUT IT ONLINE

STEP 3
MAKE IT PODCAST READY

STEP 4
TELL THE WORLD

Step 1 - Create Digital Media

Let me start by clarifying one thing - podcasting isn't only audio. Podcasting can also be video or even PDF files. Audio currently remains the most popular form of podcasting, but video is quickly catching up. Distribution of other media files, like PDF, is also possible, but has a limited appeal and audience. My focus in this book will be primarily on audio media production, but most of the strategies can be adapted for other types of podcasts as well.

So what is the difference between a podcast and just making digital media available online? In short, podcasting provides a digital "wrapper" around your online media that makes it accessible to all podcasting clients, enabling extra benefits like syndication and subscription. We'll discuss those in detail in the next chapters. The first step is simply to make the media, so that we can put a podcast wrapper around it.

It might seem a bit redundant to say "digital" media since almost all media is digital these days, but I wanted to start at the very beginning and stay true to my promise — that this book is newbie-friendly. It is actually possible to take existing audio tapes and make them into a podcast, although I've only known a few people who have done it. Most people reading this book will want to make new content for their podcast, so that is what I'm going to cover here. In this chapter I'm also going to explain how to make digital media even if you don't have a microphone or a camera.

If you are interested in podcasting video, check out my book *How to Stream Video Live* 2016 for more information on creating compelling video content.

Digital Audio in Two Steps

Step 1: Record And Edit Your Video

Step one is simple: just record and edit your audio on your phone, iPad or your computer. When you are satisfied with every single aspect of your audio, including production, editing and enhancing, you can go on to step two.

Step 2: Convert Your Audio file to an MP3.

You're probably familiar already with the Mp3 format. It's pretty standard for audio files, and can be shared and played anywhere. That's it!

Now, the specifics...

Is All Digital Media a Podcast?

You may be asking yourself, "What's the difference between a podcast and other online media, such as a YouTube video or a media file on my website?"

Great question.

At the core of it, any digital media you create can be used to produce YouTube videos, CDs, streaming radio shows and more. It is the same media — it's just what you do with the media that makes it a podcast. In terms of file format, it is all the same thing.

So in this step, forget about podcasting. You are simply creating digital media to use any way you want. I call that process *multicasting*.

Making Digital Media Right Now

If you're reading this book, the chances are very high that you have a smartphone. You might even be reading this book on one right now. Honestly, that's all you need to make a digital recording. I have a podcast that I record almost entirely on my phone when I get stuck in traffic. More details about that particular podcast can be found here: http://PaulColligan.com/TOLCast

Yes, all I need to do to make that podcast happen is to talk into my phone. I often record while driving and running errands. I usually use a pair of $9.99 earbuds because that's all I tend to have in the car with me when I record an episode.

I told you, this doesn't need to be complicated.

Believe it or not, there are a number of surprisingly good smartphone programs that record audio. So many, in fact, that I hesitate to list any specific one here. One great combo microphone-and-software package that works on both iPhone and Android devices is called the iRig Mic Cast: http://PaulColligan.com/PhoneMic

Will you have a high-fidelity, perfect-sounding podcast using just your phone? No. But you don't always need a high-fidelity, perfect-sounding podcast. Sometimes, good enough is good enough. I've had clients whose podcast episodes have hundreds of thousands of downloads, and they were recorded just this way.

If you don't have a smartphone, or don't really want to use one to record your content, there are plenty of ways to record directly to your computer. In addition to your computer, you will need a USB computer microphone and an audio recording program.

My favorite computer microphone right now is the "Nessie" by Blue, and it works on both Apple and Windows machines. That could change at any time (my preference I mean — the microphone will always work on both operating systems), but the following link will always take you to my current recommendation.

http://PaulColligan.com/Nessie

Another more powerful option is the iRig iMic HD

http://PaulColligan.com/iRigiMicHD

Some of the computer microphones today record surprisingly well and can help you sound a lot better than you might think possible.

If you are recording directly to your computer, my favorite audio recording program is Audacity. It's free and it also works on both Apple and Windows machines.

http://PaulColligan.com/Audacity

There are plenty of other choices to record audio, so just pick one and start recording. *Don't get lost in sorting through all of the options.* Remember, millions of hours of successful podcasts have been listened to with less technology than I've listed above. Trust me — you don't need to make this complicated.

For a video tutorial of recording audio on the iRig Mic Cast, visit this link:

http://PaulColligan.com/AudioOnMicCast

To see how I record "Thinking Out Loud" using nothing but my iPhone, visit this link:
http://PaulColligan.com/HowIRecordTOL

Here's another bonus video for you: "How To Record And Edit Audio on Your Computer with Audacity and the Nessie USB Microphone"

http://PaulColligan.com/AudacityNessie

Audio Recording Made Easy

No Extra Equipment or Fancy Software Needed

As I write these paragraphs, I can already hear in my head some pundits composing their rebuttal to what I am about to recommend. However, it all goes back to that simple question: Why do some people try to make podcasting more complicated than it needs to be?

One simple way to record audio is to use a service that hosts conference calls. There are a number of companies that provide conference-call services for little to no cost, and many of them will record the call for you as well. It's an easy way to record podcast audio, including interviews with participants in other locations.

At the time of this writing, UberConference (http://PaulColligan.com/UberConference) has a free service with great audio quality. This offer is subject to change, but even their $10-per-month offering is currently well worth your money. You simply call into the service and chat as usual, and the system records the call for you.

You may also be wondering: "Doesn't audio recorded on a phone bridge sound like audio recorded on a phone bridge?" Yes, it does — but that doesn't always matter. The very popular and excellent "I Love Marketing" podcast (http://PaulColligan.com/ILoveMarketing) gets thousands of downloads a day, and is often recorded in this very way. Dean Jackson, the show's co-host, calls it the "No-Click Podcast."

More Advanced: The Recording Matrix

Not every Podcast is as easy as recording the individual in the room. Sometimes you want to record an interview with someone in a different physical location. There are lots of options but they can be confusing and frustrating - and aren't always reliable. I'd like to attempt to make things a bit simpler here.

The attached Recording Matrix is a list of the many options and my thoughts on each.

Most of these are self explanatory - but let me define one concept that isn't common: the "Double Ender" technique refers to the practice of using great microphones on each side of the conversation, even if it's being recorded with a lower-fidelity technology, such as a phone or VOIP. This will help the editor line up the different files. It's a powerful technique for getting great audio with a lesser chance of technology failure. It's not perfect, but it's the most foolproof option so far.

The ability to record a remote interview is pretty cool. Obviously, if you have a system that already works for you, use it, but if you are looking for options, consider the information in the following chart.

PODCAST INTERVIEW RECORDING MATRIX 1.1

Technique	Ease Of Use	Audio Quality	Reliability	More Info	Final Verdict
Double Ender	Difficult	Excellent	Excellent	HowToPodcast Book.com	If both sides are comfortable with the process, this creates the best possible recording.
Skype Recording	Difficult To Set Up. Somewhat Easy To Use	Based On Quality of Skype Call	Often Unreliable	Ecamm.com/mac/callrecorder/ (Mac) TotalRecorder.com/ (Windows) etc.	Skype recorders are great when the software and Skype are working well. The unreliable nature of both make this a less than perfect technique.
Phone Bridgeline Recording	Easy	Quality Of A Phone Call	Excellent	DialTalkDone.com Uberconference.com etc.	Provides a reliable recording option with no technical skills or gear required.
Interview Apps / Services	From Easy To Difficult Based On App / Service	Variable	Not Reliable	Zencastr.com etc.	Although a great concept, there are no apps / services that we can recommend at this point.
Remove Audio From Video Recording	Depends On System Used For Video Recording	Depends On System Used For Video Recording / Quality Of Connection During Recording	Depends On Reliability Of Service Used	HangOuts.Google.com Zoom.us etc.	If you are comfortable with the reliability of the service and the quality of the audio and your participants are comfortable with the tech, this is a solid option.

Editing Digital Media

Now, assuming you've made some digital media and it isn't perfect. What can you do? There is a whole debate about what is "good enough" in terms of quality, but we won't deal with that here. Many of you will still want to edit after you've created your audio, and that's understandable.

Fortunately, many of the programs used to record digital media can also be used to edit digital media. If you think of them like a word processor for media, you'll be in a good place. Put in your initial content, then edit it so that it's as clean and mistake-free as possible.

Audacity, the company I recommended earlier, is also a great, *simple* platform for editing audio. There are lots of choices, but I like going with simple. This is what my team uses to edit ALL of my podcasts right now. The simpler the program, the easier it is going to be to edit. You're not going for major awards here; your goal is to get your point across in a way that's as easy to access as possible.

Is the volume not quite right? Is there an annoying audio hum that you need to get rid of? We'll cover a very easy solution to that problem. Pay special attention to everything I have to say about the cloud solution Auphonic a little later on.

Another possibility for getting your audio edited is to outsource it. You might be thinking "Isn't that incredibly expensive?" It can be, but there are some interesting services available in the international marketplace. Take a look at Fiverr (http://PaulColligan.com/Fiverr) and search for "audio editing." It's amazing what kind of work you can get done for $5. I've personally used this service many, many times. Obviously, *buyer-beware* for this or any other discount service, but it can be a great option. Other services that are a little less "bottom of the barrel" include UpWork (http://PaulColligan.com/UpWork) and People Per Hour (http://PaulColligan.com/PeoplePerHour).

New: Dial Talk Done

If this all seems a little too time consuming for you, consider our new service called Dial-Talk-Done. Below is a graphic that explains how it works. Basically, the name says it all. It isn't for everyone, but those we're testing it with LOVE IT. It's quick and easy Podcasting in three short steps.

Even if you don't use or consider Dial Talk Done, it's a great example of how easy podcasting can be. While this book explains Podcasting in four steps, Dial Talk Done brings it down to three.

Step one: Call the number for Dial-Talk-Done.

Step two: Identify yourself and speak your podcast, right from your phone.

Step three: When you are satisfied with your recording, the voice prompts will ask for your podcast title, description, desired date of publication, and any edits you would like made. Complete the process and your part is done.

It doesn't get any easier than that!

If you are concerned about the fidelity issues of a phone call, there are some simple ways you can send in a better quality audio file.

Visit http://DialTalkDone.com for more information.

www.DialTalkDone.com

No hardware or software required. All participants (co-hosts, interviewees, etc.) call into your unique DTD phone number.

DIAL

TALK

All calls will be automatically recorded. Speak your show, interview, update, etc.

Fill out a short form with episode details after you hang up. Don't want to fill out a form? Call a second time with episode specifics.

DONE

Episode will be live on date requested - or the next business day.

PODCAST PARTNERSHIP

New: Editing Audio With Ferrite

A new solution in the audio editing and recording world is an app called "Ferrite" from a company called, of all things "Wooji Juice." Currently it's only available on iOS.

http://PaulColligan.com/Ferrite

Two things make Ferrite worth mentioning:

1. It's a complete recording and editing solution for iOS (and only iOS at the time of writing.)
2. It will export your projects in an uncompressed format directly into the Auphonic App for leveling, tagging, etc.

This means you can record, edit and publish a Podcast using nothing but an iOS device. While this might be a bit tight on an iPhone, the same iPad Pro I'm using right now can become a complete audio Podcasting machine.

As a matter of fact, I've already changed my workflow to include recording and editing in Ferrite on my iPad and then switching to Auphonic for post production. I'll talk more about Auphonic a little later in this chapter, but basically I can do the whole thing from a coffee shop, my living room, or anywhere I can connect to WiFi.

There are several microphones that record great digital sound directly into iOS devices, including the iRig iMic HD and the Blu Nessie (when connected with the USB). Combine this with Ferrite and your iPad and you have a simple, elegant and portable solution for producing quality audio without a studio.

http://PaulColligan.com/iRigiMicHD

http://PaulColligan.com/Nessie

The one caveat here, there is still no easy way to record an interview from another program such as Skype or FaceTime from a phone or tablet device, so if you are getting content from external programs, this is not the solution for you.

New: Editing And Recording With Auphonic Recorder

The Auphonic service mentioned later in this chapter recently released a recorder app for both the iOS and Android Platforms. They are extremely simplistic in nature but provide another way to record and edit simple audio on a portable device.

Also, the Auphonic Recorder works great on the new Chromebooks that support the Android App Store and it's the best option we've found for that platform by far.

http://PaulColligan.com/AuphonicRecordiOS

http://PaulColligan.com/AuphonicRecorderAndroid

Is Editing Really Necessary?

One of the common pitfalls for new podcasters is spending too much time in the editing process. They spend a few minutes recording the content, but then get stuck in the cycle of editing, and are not willing to release the final product until it is perfect.

Striving for perfection can really work against you in podcasting. Your main goal as a podcaster is to get your message out, not sound like you were recorded in an expensive studio. Sure, you don't want to burst audience eardrums with an overly dramatic sneeze, but you should realize that leaving in the occasional "um" or pause just proves that you're a human. Focus on creating compelling and useful content, and no one will notice these little flaws.

Making Better-Sounding and Better-Looking Media

Despite what you might have heard— sounding good has very little to do with the microphone.

90% of getting a good sound depends on two things: the environment in which you are recording, and how close your mouth is to the microphone when you record. All you need to do is use a decent microphone, place it near your lips and record in a good environment, and you are almost there.

What makes a good environment for recording is pretty simple. It should be quiet. Obviously, avoid public spaces where you can't control what is happening in the room. A private room with a door in your home or office will work just fine. It doesn't have to be completely soundproof. If your neighbor is mowing his lawn or your assistant knocks on the door, it probably won't affect your recording too much.

Good acoustics are also important. You should do what you can to keep noise from bouncing around the room. Simple things like adding carpet and furniture to the room will help tremendously with sound quality. You don't want to sound like you're in a tunnel or an empty warehouse. Find a way way to dampen the echo chamber effect of a bare room. YouTube is a great source of information and videos on this process, if you need more.

If soundproofing is not an option, you can always put your microphone in a box like this one:
http://PaulColligan.com/MicBox

Or, in the worst-case scenario, you can do the very thing BBC war correspondents did during World War II: record by speaking into a microphone with a blanket over your head and the microphone. Don't knock it — it really works! I've recorded more than a dozen episodes of different shows using this technique, including an episode recorded at 2 a.m. in a London hotel room.

Adam Curry's Podcaster Pro

If you ever wondered why radio station DJs, and some Podcasts, just sound different than you do when you record, it's because they have an array of tools like compressor limiters, equalization, noise gates and more. While these tools are currently available to Podcasters, the price and technological know-how required to use them have made them inaccessible to most.

That might be changing. Adam Curry, one of the inventors of podcasting, introduced a product early in 2017 called Podcaster Pro. Essentially, this product is a box, about the size of a big hardbound book that allows you to plug in a standard XLR microphone and get the power of these professional recording tools in one simple device. PodcasterPro will NOT work with USB microphones.

In short, plug in a mic and get the studio sound you've always wanted. While the technology represented by the Podcaster Pro is nothing new, the ease of use and reasonable price requires serious consideration from any aspiring podcaster.

In addition, the tools makes it possible to bring the enhanced technology to Skype for remote interviews, so you can sound your best if you're being interviewed for someone else's show.

Truth be told, I don't have access to the box yet, but I know the team behind it and have been impressed with everything I've seen so far. I ordered my early access version on the first day of the campaign and will update this book with more details as soon as I can.

Hint: Make sure you register your book to get the update when I write it.

http://PaulColligan.com/PodcasterPro

Auphonic

As I mentioned earlier, Auphonic is my podcasting secret weapon. This is the tool I personally use to optimize my recorded sound files and convert them to MP3 format. Auphonic is so powerful because it saves you valuable time in editing while still delivering a high quality result. We used to spend an hour or so optimizing our audio manually. Now, we just run it through Auphonic and it sounds better than it ever used to.

While Auphonic doesn't fix everything a sound engineer would, it does an amazing job with most audio and saves you a ton of time by using software to balance your recording. I highly recommend Auphonic to all aspiring podcasters.

Video - How I Optimize my Audio and Convert it to MP3 Using Auphonic

http://PaulColligan.com/AuphonicVideo

Lossless files

This next tip comes from almost a decade of cumulative experience from both my students and myself.

When you create your audio files and manage them throughout all of the editing process, keep everything in a "lossless" file format. This usually means a ".WAV" or ".AIFF" file.

Why? When you edit compressed media, it always loses a bit of sound quality in the process. If you don't want that problem, you can get around it by editing your files in a lossless format.

Literally, LESS sound quality is LOST during the editing process by using a LOSSLESS format. Easy to remember, right?

The FINAL step in editing a podcast is to convert it into the MP3 file. If you're looking for specifics, I like using **96 kbps Mono MP3 file** These should be an option in whatever audio program you are using for editing. An MP3 file compresses the data for easier transfer and storage, so doing this step last will ensure the best possible quality.

Making Media Without a Camera or Microphone

Many people have asked me about using a voice-to-text program to take existing articles or blog posts and convert them directly into an audio podcast. While I love leveraging technology, this just isn't a reality yet. Although it's technically possible, the software isn't sophisticated enough yet to convey what you are trying to say in an effective or interesting way. It's still going to sound like a computer reading an article, and nobody wants to listen to that.

However, your podcast does not necessarily have to be in your own personal speaking voice.

If you don't want to do it yourself, you can outsource the recording of the podcast to voice talent. Basically, this just involves hiring someone else to read your words. It's pretty expensive, and involves a few more steps than just clicking "record," but it's an option if you are exceptionally self-conscious about your voice or have another valid reason for doing it. Currently, I know of at least one podcast in the Top 20 on iTunes that follows this very method.

If you would like to produce a video podcast, and the thought of dealing with lights, HD cameras and skin blemishes makes you a little queasy, don't worry — there is the whole world of *Screencasting* to explore. Screencasting is basically just video content recorded from your computer screen, often in the form of Powerpoint or Keynote slideshows. Just because people want to look at something while they listen to your podcast doesn't mean it has to be your face. It's a really effective way to teach or train others with a podcast. You can show them how to do whatever you are talking about, right on the screen.

In my opinion, the best tools for screencasting are *Screenflow* on the Mac and *Camtasia* on Windows.

http://PaulColligan.com/Screenflow

http://PaulColligan.com/Camtasia

Another option I recommend is just to GET OVER IT! Part of what makes podcasting so powerful is that it's *you*, conveying *your* message, *your* passion, in *your* voice. You don't need to sound like an evening news anchor to do a podcast. Personally, whenever I hear something too perfect, polished and overproduced I get a little suspicious, or even bored. Just try to relax a little and be yourself and you'll do great.

Warning: Make Sure You Are Legal

This section could be a whole book, but the bottom line is this: don't ever use audio, video or other recorded sounds or images made by someone else in your podcast without being 100% sure that you have the full legal rights to do so.

You may think you're so small that it doesn't matter, or you may have heard the term "fair use" and think it applies to you. It doesn't.

29

I'm no lawyer, but believe me when I say this: using someone else's content in your podcast is a quick way to get yourself into a lot of trouble. Without going into details, the downloadable nature of podcasting, combined with the international availability of the internet, makes this stuff very tempting to lawyers looking for easy prey.

In addition to being illegal, it's also unethical and a really bad business practice. Create your own original content or obtain written permission to use someone else's ideas, symbols, artwork, music, etc. and always, always give credit to the original creator. You wouldn't want someone using your stuff without your permission, would you?

I should also point out that if you have content created or edited for you by someone else that contains copyrighted content, you're just as liable. If someone tells you that the audio or video they've created for you is free of copyrights and restrictions, it's a smart move to ask for some documented proof. The good ones will be willing to provide it to you.

People Come for the Podcast Content, They Stay for the Podcast Voice

This section header is a loose paraphrase of Merlin Mann and Dan Benjamin from the 5by5 network (http://PaulColligan.com/5by5), but it's an important point nonetheless.

Their idea is simple: the power of podcasting does not lie in the quality of the recording or the technology behind your MP3 file — it's in the power of the ideas and thoughts communicated by the host.

To dig a little deeper, it's not *what* you say, but *how* you say it that keeps people coming back. It's *your* voice and *your* ideas that give your podcast power, so make sure you spend more time thinking through what you want to say than on any other part of this process.

What About GarageBand, Adobe Audition or [insert fancypants audio editing program here]...?

There are plenty of other great options for recording and editing digital media than the ones I have listed, and many books and training programs are out there to teach you how to use them...but that's not the focus of this book. Expensive audio programs will not make you a better podcaster any more than an expensive knife will make you a better chef.

Now, if you are already familiar with one of these other programs, go ahead and use it — there's no need to waste any time learning something new. I just want to prevent the pain for someone out there who thinks that they need to master complicated software in order to share their message with the world. You don't.

That's It?

Yes, that's it. Step one is as simple as talking into your phone. Editing can be done quickly and easily, with powerful online tools like Auphonic doing all the heavy lifting.

Are you ready to take action? Go for it! Need a little more information? Watch the videos we've mentioned to get all the specifics. Either way, you are ready for Step two — so let's turn our attention to getting your media online.

As a special bonus, here's a worksheet from my How To Podcast Training program that puts audio file formats and the production process into a single sheet of paper for easy reference.

31

AUDIO FILE FORMATS AND THE PRODUCTION PROCESS

OVERVIEW - WIKIPEDIA

Lossless compression is a class of data compression algorithms that allows the original data to be perfectly reconstructed from the compressed data. **Lossy** compression permits reconstruction only of an approximation of the original data, which usually improves compression rates and reduces file sizes, but reduces the quality.

THINGS TO CONSIDER

Whenever possible, you want to record and edit your audio in a lossless audio file format. Although there are plenty of variables in production, a ".WAV" or ".AIFF" file is usually your best choice for audio file formats. Lossless files will be significantly larger than lossy files in size.

This is especially important when recording to portable devices such as smartphones, tablets and portable audio recorders.

Note: Taking a lossy file and making it a lossless file for production will have no affect on the quality. For the best sound quality, the audio needs to be recorded, at origin, in a lossless format.

You want to use the popular .mp3, mp4, and .m4v file formats ONLY as the last step in the production process.

THE IDEAL PRODUCTION PROCESS

Record Lossless: Record your audio in a lossless format. Use only software, services and vendors that make this option a possibility.

Edit Lossless: The entire editing process should be done, whenever possible, with lossless files. This will make for larger project files.

Finalize Lossy: Produce the final distribution file in a lossy format, but keep/archive the lossless project file for any future editing requirements.

Step 2 - Put It Online

Once you've made your digital media, you need to place it online. You should use a service that can distribute it to people around the world when they request it, and provide any podcast-specific services, if and when they are needed. This can be ridiculously cheap. You just need to have the right mindset and find the right partners. We'll set you up with those here and even get you a free month with one of our favorite services.

How Media Gets Online

For those unfamiliar with the process, let me take a few minutes to highlight a few different ways you can get your media online. The easiest way is usually to upload your MP3 file through the web interface of your media host. There are also some automated tools, like Auphonic, that will do the file transfer for you automatically as part of their process.

View the following video to see how easy it is to put your podcast media online using Libsyn.com, the host I use and recommend: (http://PaulColligan.com/Libsyn).

Free Video: Putting Podcast Media Online

http://PaulColligan.com/PutMediaOnline

Is Online the Same Thing as "The Cloud?"

I've seen a funny t-shirt that says *"No one really knows what the cloud is."* I hate to make complicated things too simple, but the "cloud" is just a hard drive or computer attached to the internet that you don't have to personally monitor or maintain.

This is exactly what you want for your online podcasting media. You want to put it on someone else's internet-connected hard drive, and you don't want to worry about a thing once you've put it there. In the cloud, your data is always available and accessible whenever and wherever you need it.

The beautiful thing about the cloud is that it is consistent and reliable, and you don't have to manage it 24/7. This is the kind of service your podcast deserves. Remember, our goal is to keep it simple and get things done. Any podcast host we recommend in this book will meet your needs and will be, for all intents and purposes, a "cloud" service.

The Right Mindset

Many of the hosting companies that offer unlimited hosting often have tiny little fine print, which basically says that online media files aren't included in their service. Also, they often host media in a way that iTunes will simply reject.

In some cases, you won't get caught and iTunes won't care. But if your show ends up doing a lot of business, you could get shut down quickly. Nothing is worse than seeing your podcast finally get the attention it deserves, and then finding out that your host has shut you down as a result.

Many people ask me "Can I use free hosting?" In terms of free hosting, you, my friend, can do whatever you want. However, the old phrase "You get what you pay for," is as true of podcast hosting as it is anywhere else. You want a partner who can handle the traffic when it happens, and keep the big players happy.

Even though it may not be free, reliable media hosting does not need to be expensive. There is a whole industry of media hosting that is extremely affordable, with some options starting as low as $5 a month. Your podcast hosting doesn't need to be a burden or an out-of-control expense, but you should pay a few bucks to do it right.

The Right Partners

There is no need to do this on your own. I recommend you seek out strategic partners in your podcasting efforts. The right kind of partners - i.e., partners who have been there before, have success under their belts and have a strategic reason to offer their services to you.

Technology partners have come a long way in the last ten years. There are a number of great candidates who meet the podcast hosting requirements I write about and even provide feed-authoring services as well. One of the best things about not being first at this game is that you don't need to make the mistakes others have made. Join up with a technology partner that has already done what you are hoping to do. I list a few excellent partners in the next section of this chapter. They can save you a great deal of time and effort and are very affordable.

Beware all-in-one marketing partners who claim they have a system or technology that will help you make your podcast, promote it, get advertisers for it, help you generate revenue and more. In short, I've never seen an all-in-one technology with a model that works in the real world. In my experience, I've never seen it work successfully — and I doubt you will either.

If it seems to be too go to be true, it probably is.

If you are going to bring on a consulting partner, make sure they've had success previously with someone in your same situation. Podcasting is over a decade old now - you don't need to be anyone's guinea pig. Just because someone knows how to make a Podcast doesn't mean they know how to make a profitable one.

What is a Byte-Range Request, and Does it Matter?

ATTENTION: IMPORTANT NERD ALERT

Apple now requires that servers serving media files have something called "byte-range requests" enabled. Make sure your podcast host has this feature; everyone we recommend in this book does.

Who We Recommend for Your Hosting Technology Partner

You want to put your media on a host specifically designed for podcasts. The only host I recommend now is Libsyn.com, which has prices as low as $5 a month. You just can't beat that deal for quality hosting. http://PaulColligan.com/Libsyn

And, if you use the coupon code "Paul" you'll get your first month for free!

How good are they? Libsyn hosts ALL of my podcasts as well as the podcasts of all of my clients. At this point in the game there is simply no other choice. If something new pops up, I'll let you know (as long as you register your book).

How Can Unlimited Hosting Be Real?

I'm going to take some time here to deal with an issue that any thinking person needs to examine. How can someone offer unlimited hosting for such low prices? Is it really unlimited? Can you trust it?

It's all about the math and the economy of scale.

While no one can give you true unlimited hosting without losing money, especially at the low, low rates some hosts charge, very few podcasts are capable of generating the kind of traffic that will cost the hosting company money. It's the same idea behind offering unlimited voice minutes on cell phone family plans these days. My two teenage daughters use about five minutes of their unlimited voice minutes on their phones during any given month. Since most teenagers text and rarely use voice, it really isn't costing the service provider very much to offer unlimited voice, (although texting is another story).

Essentially, hosting companies buy storage in bulk at a discount and bank on the fact that very few podcasts are as popular as their creators want them to be. They make up their revenue in volume. So, while there are some podcasts that represent a monthly financial loss to any hosting company, there are still enough that don't, so they can continue to afford to offer hosting at competitive prices and still make money.

Will we see unlimited hosting options forever? I'm betting yes, but I can't tell you for sure. Hosting and bandwidth are getting cheaper every day, so it would take significant industry changes for this option to disappear.

About Reporting And Statistics

There is a lot that can be said about reporting statistics, but we're trying to keep things simple here. In short, the way hosting companies traditionally manage and track files simply doesn't work in podcasting. There are plenty of articles about this fact online if you want to look it up.

What does this mean to you? Well, it means that you'll want reporting specifically designed for podcasting and the unique issues it brings. Libsyn (http://PaulColligan.com/Libsyn), mentioned earlier, has a great reporting package included in their program. Another good option is the stats program offered by Blubrry (http://PaulColligan.com/Blubrry).

Many people who are making their first foray into the podcasting space are disappointed to realize how limited the podcasting stats actually are. The very nature of the downloadable media file delivered via a podcast means that you don't get information on how many times a specific file was downloaded, or if it was listened to, or even for how long it was listened to. No matter what you've heard, podcast reporting is limited to what was downloaded, where it was downloaded and what technologies were used in the process. This limitation is something all podcasters have to deal with no matter how successful they are.

Again, this isn't something you need to worry about. The data you can get from podcast reporting is still phenomenal — it just may not be as complete as you had hoped.

One interesting thing to note about podcasting stats is that companies such as Stitcher (http://PaulColligan.com/Stitcher), which offer streaming services, can deliver a few more stats about your podcast, at least in terms of how it plays to their audience.

What Happens if I Have to Change Media Hosts?

Common sense dictates that you should keep a backup of your podcast episodes, and I encouraged you to do that in step one. If you archive well, you can navigate the worst-case scenario of changing hosts pretty easily. All you will have to do is take your most recent archive, move it, and then point your podcast audience to the new host.

This mobility illustrates the beauty of the podcasting infrastructure. You can pick up and move your podcast, just like you can pick up and move from one mobile phone company to another.

Pick a Host and Move On to the Next Chapter

That's all there is for step two. Pick a host that makes sense for you and get your media online.

Once you have your media online with a smart host, you're ready for the next step: making your content podcast-ready. See how easy this is?

Step 3 - Make it Podcast-Ready

Now we're getting to the part that elevates this process from simply creating online media to creating a podcast. A *podcast feed* is the heart of what makes it possible for you to podcast your media so people can subscribe to it. Like the earlier steps, you'll need the right mindset and the right partners if you want to get it done quickly, without unnecessary complication.

Don't worry - we're not going to get too technical here. A feed is simply what you need to make your content podcast-ready. That's why I named this chapter after the end result, not the process. Another way to think of it is this: A device that stores and plays a podcast is called a *podcast client*. A client could be an iPhone, an MP3 player, or your computer. The *podcast feed* contains all the directions that a podcast client needs to have to make it all work. A podcast feed is pretty quick and easy to make, *if you do it right.* Part of your podcast feed is created from data already found in your album art information which we'll also cover later in this chapter.

This should be the shortest step of your podcasting journey. Your only job here is to pick the right partner for this process and then move on to your content production. If this isn't the shortest chapter in the book, or you spend any time worrying about this step, I've done something wrong.

How Does Online Media Become "Podcast-Ready?"

A little behind-the-scenes fact: podcast (RSS) feeds are in a file format called XML. XML is something that is read only by computers and, as a result, should only be generated, automatically, by a computer. Think of XML the same way you think of *Postscript* the file format your computer uses to tell the printer how to print something. *That's right: a Microsoft Word doc, a PDF viewer or any other file you send to the printer uses a special language only the geekiest of nerds know how to program in - and you probably didn't even know it existed.* Approach XML and your podcast feed in the same way; it's something that computers create, not you.

So, all we're going to do is find a computer to write your podcast feed for you, so that you can focus on creating the content. Fair enough?

Once you finish the process of setting up a feed, it is truly a "set-it-and-forget-it" system. You can leave alone and not worry about for a single moment, ever again. Once you've done this correctly, the world is automatically updated with everything they need to know about your podcast, including updates when new episodes are released.

If you're a bit more technologically savvy and you're wondering if feeds for blogs and feeds for podcasts are the same thing, the answer is, in many ways, yes. Feeds for podcasts have additional information related to the media attached, and have a few variables that allow *podcatchers* (such as iTunes) to give some content specifically related to podcasting.

What Does a Feed Look Like?

A feed file is accessible over the internet with a web address, usually in some version of the form: http://www.domain.com/feed.rss.

Straight, untranslated RSS is hard for a human to decipher, although some systems will produce a more human-friendly interpretation of an RSS feed. Such an approach is unnecessary from a technical standpoint, but it prevents some people from thinking that something is broken when they click on a URL associated with your podcast and see nothing but code.

Where Do Feeds Come From?

Feeds are basically produced in three different ways:

Option 1: *Many podcasting hosts such as Libsyn generate your feed automatically.* If this is the path you choose, it is more than enough, and allows you to work on content instead of analyzing XML. I like this option a lot because, simply, it lets the computer do the stuff that computers are good at doing.

Option 2: *Most blogging platforms such as WordPress generate basic RSS feeds by* default. (http://PaulColligan.com/WordPress) Believe it or not, in most cases, the feed produced automatically by linking to a media file in your blog is enough to work with iTunes, although it isn't optimized to deliver a great presentation. There are WordPress plugins you can use such as PowerPress (http://PaulColligan.com/PowerPress) that will refine the process slightly and allow you to deliver all of the information that iTunes is looking for.

Option 3: *The last option is to write the feed yourself.* I can't tell you how much I hate this approach. I find it to be the stuff bad science fiction stories are made of; when we do the work that the robots should be doing, the robots win.

In my opinion, you should no more write your own XML then you should write the Postscript file for the shopping list that you send to the printer. However, there are some control freaks who insist on doing it themselves, and occasionally there is a business reason for doing so (although this is a .01% kind of thing). If you believe you need to do this, I suggest two things: double check again that there isn't a tool that meets your needs, and don't let the person in charge of writing the code produce the content for your podcast. It's unlikely they'll be good at doing both.

In my batch of free videos associated with this book, you'll notice a video called "How A Podcast Host Makes My RSS So I Don't Have To" (http://PaulColligan.com/MakesMyRSS). That video walks you through the process I use for one of my podcasts.

Why iTunes Comes First in Podcast Feeds

If you're wondering how in the world you can make a single feed that works in iTunes, and in Stitcher, and for Microsoft machines, and for *the other 100 options that make podcasting so exciting*, I have some great news for you. Thanks to the beautiful work already done by Apple, the reality is simple:

All you need to do to make sure your podcast feed works everywhere is to make sure that it works on iTunes.

Every podcast client tracks and monitors what Apple is doing, and makes sure that whatever you put in your feed (for the sake of Apple), works on their system as well. Use this to your advantage and quickly make a feed that works on iTunes — and then get back to creating your content.

New: Advanced Tagging In Podcast Feeds

In June 2017, Apple announced new features for their Podcasts app to be released with iOS 11 later in the year. The app will now give the option to download an entire season, rather than just one episode at a time. You will also be able to set the order that your episodes are downloaded in.

All of these features are made possible through specific tags in your Podcast feed. At the time this was written, Libsyn fully supports the ability to add additional tags to your Podcasts episodes and shows and will fully support these features. I expect the other Podcast hosts to follow quickly.

Once we understand more about these options, we'll update the book with specifics. To make sure you are updated when we do, please register your copy of the book at http://HowToPodcastBook.com.

Why You *Must* Control Your Feed

The web address for your feed is how the world, and the podcast directories, know how to find you. If you suddenly have to change feeds, it's difficult to let the world know you've moved. Although there are ways to migrate one feed to another, it's very complicated, time consuming, not 100% effective, and rarely works as planned.

Think of your podcast feed in the same way that you think of your mobile phone number. Just as you should never sign up with a phone service provider who won't explain what happens to your number if you ever leave their service, never work with a feed provider who isn't crystal clear that *you own your feed* and can do what you want with it. When you own the phone number, you can hop from one provider to another without anyone having to know. Moving your podcast feed, should you ever need to, should be just as simple.

Many hosts give you the chance to use their service and link it with your domain, so you'd have a feed along the lines of: http://www.yourdomain.com/yourfeed.rss. This is the smartest move. Why? Because if you have to move from one host or service to another, the world doesn't need to know. Obviously, if you're using a tool to create the feed on your own domain, you don't need to worry about this.

I'll be blunt: there are some providers who, once they create the feed for your show, own that feed. They usually host it on their own domain, which makes it almost impossible for you to ever leave them. Sometimes they do it on purpose, sometimes they are just being lazy. Either way it's a bad move, and you want to stay away from them. I have a great alternative for you later in this chapter (Feedburner), but stay away from this other type of provider if at all possible.

About Album Art (or Podcast Art)

Podcasting started because of the MP3 player, and from day one it has mimicked the infrastructure already set in place for that platform to make things work smoothly. For a podcast, the terms are simply changed to "Show Title" instead of "Album Name", and what were once called "Tracks" are now called "Episodes." Yes, the average album might have 10 "Episodes," but there is no set limit. So don't worry, nothing will break when you pass episode number 200.

When you open up any podcatching program (such as iTunes), you'll notice that all podcasts have square artwork to represent each podcast. This also comes from the MP3 player world, and is equivalent to "Album Art" in an MP3 player. Just like Taylor

Swift's Album *1989* has a distinctive piece of album art, your podcast can have its own unique podcast art.

Podcast art should be square, simply because that's the format the industry expects from albums. At the time of publication, iTunes wants your album art to be at least 1400 x 1400 pixels, but they currently support up to 3000 x 3000. We recommend you submit your art as 3000 x 3000 as that will become the standard soon. You need to place it online in either the JPG or PNG format. It really doesn't matter which one you pick, whatever format your artwork comes in will be fine.

There are a number of simple ways to create album art. One of the easiest is the web application Canva (http://PaulColligan.com/Canva). The program has templates that you can quickly customize to your needs.

Another option is to get your album art custom designed. How much does this cost? Well, obviously, you can pay as much as you want, but a little-known site called Fiverr (http://PaulColligan.com/Fiverr — note the two R's) offers a marketplace of people who will do things for just five dollars. Truth be told, I've had most of my podcast album art created with one of their vendors. I love the world economy!

Finally, the question: "Can I make my own album art?" Yes, of course you can. But iTunes is filled with podcasts that no one takes seriously, because their album art screams "LOOK, SOMEONE WITH NO REAL GRAPHICS SKILLS MADE THIS!" If that's how you design (it's definitely how I design), stay away from making your own graphics. The old adage "you never get a second chance to make a first impression" is certainly relevant here. Since your album art is the first introduction your audience gets to your podcast, make sure it's a good one.

The Right Mindset

I hinted at this at the beginning of the chapter, but *please* — don't spend too much time on this. For 99% of you, your podcast host will write your feed, and for the rest of you, there are ridiculously easy ways to get it written for you.

The Feedburner Option

In previous editions of this book I wrote about a service called Feedburner. In short, I no longer recommend this service, because the benefits it provides are no longer worth the effort.

If you don't know what Feedburner is, don't worry — it just isn't needed anymore.

A good host (such as Libsyn) offers you the chance to host your feed on your own domain name. That is an incredible insurance policy in case anything goes wrong. If your host doesn't offer that option, find a host that does.

How Do I Know If my Feed is Working?

Since iTunes is the 800-pound gorilla of podcasting, most of you reading this book will have a copy installed on your computer. For the few of you who don't, install a copy now. You are going to need it to test and submit your feed to iTunes. I'll show you how to do this in the next chapter.

On occasion, I meet people who don't want to install iTunes on their computer for one reason or another. My advice: get over it. If you are going to play in a field where iTunes is the big player, you have to make sure your stuff work with iTunes.

Now that we got that over with, you can test your feed to see if it is working in iTunes by selecting the *Subscribe to Podcast* menu option and cutting and pasting your feed into the box iTunes provides. If it works in iTunes, then your feed is fully functional. I've made a quick video of the process at http://PaulColligan.com/iTunesCheck. If iTunes changes the wording or the process, I'll make sure to update the video at that link.

Do I Need a Feed Validator?

If you've done any research in the podcasting space, you might have read about feed validators. These are programs that check your feed to make sure that there is nothing wrong with it. The most diligent of podcasters and tech-types will insist that you run your feed through a feed validator to make sure that all is well before you unleash your podcast on the public.

I've received emails from people telling me that my feed is not validated and has errors. In my opinion, the feed doesn't need to be validated, and I'm a little concerned about people who enjoy testing the feeds of others and reporting their findings — but that's another story altogether.

In my experience (gained from downloading millions of podcast episodes), a feed validator is simply overkill. While I've seen books written on this subject that disagree, here's my take: If your feed is invalid but it still works, it doesn't matter! If people can still find your podcast, it's good enough. There are no feed validator cops out there issuing citations for invalid feeds! If you use one of the services I've suggested, you'll never have to worry about this happening anyway.

With that said and done, if you are one of those check-everything-before-you-go-live types, there is no harm in running your feed through a validator — so have at it.

As I write this, there will probably be someone giving me a one-star review on Amazon, simply because of this section. Who knows, it might be you. If it isn't you and you've found the review I write of, nothing would do my heart more good than a response written by someone whose podcast is live and running because this book taught them how to focus on the stuff that really matters.

There It Is....

So, your media has been created and your feed is live. Now we need to tell a few people, especially iTunes about it, so that you can start building the audience that you deserve. On to the next chapter!

Step 4 - Tell the World

First off — and I need to say this right out — this is NOT a book about marketing your podcast. This book is simply, as promised in the title, a book on "How To Podcast." Telling the world is part of that process.

This chapter is ONLY about getting the word out about your podcast in general so that when people are looking for you, they can find you. You'll probably want to do more than is explained in this book eventually, but in these next few pages I will give you everything you need to tell the world that your podcast exists. From there, go nuts with your promotion!

When you register this book (http://HowToPodcastBook.com), I'll make sure to send you some additional content about marketing your show that expands on the concepts mentioned here.

With that said and done, let's get to work on telling the world about your podcast!

Telling the World (and Tell Them to Subscribe While You're At It)

Telling the world about your podcast really comes down to two different steps: informing the directories that your show exists, and letting your own audience know that you have a podcast they should be listening to.

By the way, don't just tell your audience that you have a podcast — tell them to *subscribe* to your podcast so that they can be informed every time you release a new episode. If you don't tell them to subscribe to the podcast, who will?

And of course, once you've made fans, tell them to spread the word about your show.

As the potential reach for your audience expands to new destinations like the connected Google Home, Alexa, or Apple HomePod connected speakers, make sure you let everyone know not just that you have a Podcast, but there are many ways to listen.

What Happens When I Release a New Episode?

Part of the beauty of podcasting is that it is a set-it-and-forget-it kind of thing. When you release a new episode, you don't need to do a single thing for others to receive it. The RSS feed you set up in the previous chapter automatically gets updated in the process of publishing, and the podcatching clients (such as iTunes) check on a regular basis and download or alert your audience as soon as they find something new. You don't have to do a thing.

I can't stress enough how cool this is. Whenever I release an episode of any of my podcasts, I've got people downloading it before I'm done finishing up the process — and as you see here, it's not a complicated process to close out. Literally within minutes of uploading my podcast to my host, I've got people all around the world downloading it.

The mechanics are all there — now you just need an audience to take advantage of them.

iTunes

iTunes is Apple's podcast directory. Different people with different agendas will tell you different numbers in terms of how many podcasts are downloaded through the iTunes directory (I've heard ranges from 60% to 95%), but there are two facts about this that are important to remember.

First, iTunes is *the* standard directory and will bring you many more times the amount of traffic than all the other directories combined. Get in iTunes before you do anything else.

Second, iTunes is one of the easiest directories to submit your podcast to. It is a two minute process maximum, and here is a great video that will walk you through the procedure: http://PaulColligan.com/SubmitToItunes

So, first things first: submit your podcast to iTunes, ONCE, and enjoy the benefits that come from it. Lately, Apple has been indexing podcasts submitted to iTunes in just a few days.

The Other Directories and Players

iTunes is not the only game in town, but it is the powerhouse of the podcasting industry. A number of other podcast clients grab their database content from iTunes (some legitimately, and some not so much), so just submitting there will get you almost everywhere you need to be.

There are a few other players in the podcast directory space that you'll want to pay attention to. However, I'm not going to list everybody with a directory because, quite simply, being listed in every available directory doesn't really matter.

Note: if you register this book, as I encouraged you to do at the beginning (http://www.HowToPodcastBook.com), and a new important podcast directory arises, I'll be sure to let you know.

Stitcher

The most fascinating podcast play outside of iTunes is, in my opinion, Stitcher. Their integration into millions of car stereo systems, and their position as one of the top choices for Android users (tablet and otherwise), makes them a directory that your show needs to be on. The following link will explain how to get your podcast listed in Stitcher:
http://PaulColligan.com/GetOnStitcher

TuneIn

At the time of writing, the market penetration of TuneIn is not that exciting at all. In my experience, only a tiny percentage of listeners come from TuneIn. They are worth mentioning because of their positioning in car stereo systems, and because this is the only big name that supports Windows phones. The number of users I see coming from TuneIn across any of the podcasts I have the stats for are, honestly, less than 1%. But Microsoft is upping their game, and the submission process is easy, so you can try it and see.

http://PaulColligan.com/GetOnTuneIn

I do have to mention that, at the time of writing, the Tesla electric car currently uses TuneIn as their podcasting client of choice. Again, I don't see any real numbers coming from TuneIn, but I do like the idea that, should Elon Musk want to listen to me, I've made it possible.

One more fascinating bit about TuneIn - it is also default on ALL of the Amazon Alexa devices. it's a bit clunky in implementation, getting your Podcast on TuneIn also means that it's available on Alexa.

iHeartRadio

In episode number ten of my show *The Podcast Report* (http://PaulColligan.com/TPR10), I interviewed Dave Jackson from The School Of Podcasting (http://PaulColligan.com/SOP) about how he got his show into iHeartRadio. I followed his direction and got The Podcast Report into iHeartRadio as well (http://PaulColligan.com/TPRIHR) — so the process works. If you want your show on iHeartRadio, listen to that episode. There are a few steps in the process, but I think it's worth it.

Since that episode, Libsyn has made it possible to submit to iHeart Radio directly through their system. There are a few steps in the process, but contact them directly to see how to get your show on iHeart.

Some of you reading this will be surprised that iHeartRadio supports podcasts, while others will wonder why in the world you'd want your new media podcast listed in such an outdated directory. In short, listen to the interview with Dave for all of the reasons. But you should realize that iHeartRadio has spent millions advertising the platform — and you, my friend, can be found there as well.

I often joke from the stage that my Mom still believes that she can't listen to my shows because she doesn't own an iPod....but she *does* have iHeartRadio installed on her Android tablet.

SoundCloud

Warning: A quick search of recent news related to SoundCloud will show you that they are having some serious financial problems and many pundits predict Soundcloud's imminent demise. As with everything in life, buyer beware.A number of podcasters have their show on SoundCloud (http://PaulColligan.com/SoundCloud). My research has shown that this option brings a minimal amount of listens, but it is still worth a paragraph or two here. SoundCloud is very interactive and very popular right now, and you might want to have your podcast associated with that brand. In addition, SoundCloud has a podcast hosting service. However, at this point, I can't recommend it.

The first thing that needs to be understood about SoundCloud is that it is not a directory. It is a separate service, sort of like the YouTube of audio. Simply said, if you don't use them as your podcast host (and I STRONGLY recommend that you don't), you'll need to upload your audio podcasts to SoundCloud every time you publish an episode to your podcast host.

They do have a free option, but anyone with any significant body of work will probably need to pay for a premium account to host their podcast at SoundCloud.

If you are carefully tracking your podcast downloads, remember that because SoundCloud pulls from their own library, you'll want to add your SoundCloud stats to whatever tracking you are doing.

To be honest, I don't currently host any of my shows at SoundCloud. However, I do have clients who host there.

Google Play Music

Google launched its own directory in 2016 by putting Podcasts inside of Google Play Music - their online music engine and service with apps for iOS and Android. Submission to Google Play Music is simple - as seen in this video.

http://PaulColligan.com/SubmitToGoogle

Google Play Music is, for lack of a better description, "The iTunes For Google Devices," without the apps and digital books. Almost anyone with an Android device has access to the store. At the time of publication, Podcasting was only available on Android devices using Google Play Music and not on the iOS release.

What is the impact of Podcasts in Google Play music? Probably tiny. It is important to note, that although Google holds the highest percentage of "smart" devices, the significant numbers are largely from low-end devices, not typically associated with media consumption. Right now, I doubt the Google Play Music directory, as it currently exists, will have any significant impact on the industry, but the size of Google's and the massive amounts of Android devices dictate that I put it here.

There are rumors of a reboot to Google's strategy for Podcasting involving YouTube, but they are, at least at the time of writing, rumors. I think this is a great idea, but time will tell.

It is also important to note that although the Kindle Fire devices from Amazon are, technically, Android devices, they have a different "store," managed by Amazon. At this point, no Amazon Podcast Directory or Client has been announced.

In my opinion, the most important benefit of getting your Podcast in Google Play Music is that shows submitted now work on the Google Home connected speakers. At this time, the Google

Home Podcast interface is more user friendly than Alexa and has the potential to make a considerable market impact.

Google Search

You don't just want to have your podcast in the directories. You want to make sure Google and the other directories know that your podcast exists, so that when someone enters your name or topic into the search engines, the website for your podcast shows up. It's just common sense.

The great thing about Google is that you really don't have to do anything anymore to let Google know that you exist. Once some other site somewhere links to you, Google will find you and index your site as well. Just linking to your site when you submit your podcast to iTunes will do the trick.

If you want a quick way to get Google to index your podcast website, write a post in Google+ which links to your site — Google will do the rest.

Amazon Alexa, Google Home, and The Apple HomePod (Connected Speakers)

One of the most interesting changes in the industry since the last release of this book is the rise of the connected speaker. I personally am listening to a lot more shows by telling my Google Home (or Alexa) what I want to listen to. These devices have made Podcast consumption as easy as telling a device what you want to hear.

Although Apple's HomePod device is over half a year away, it shows us that every major player in this space is moving to a world where we consume content, not by clicking buttons, but through voice controls.

I write about these devices here because I see the potential they have to make your podcast available to people who wouldn't know how to search for it online. Earlier I mentioned that my own mother didn't think she could listen to my Podcast because she "didn't have an Apple." Now all she has to do is tell Alexa what she wants to hear and it will play without her pushing a single button.

When you are telling the world about your Podcast, make sure they know that these connected speakers are an easy way to find you.

What About Directory Or Product "X" That You Didn't List?

There are hundreds of podcast directories. In my opinion (and hey, it's my book), once you pass the ones listed here, you simply don't get the return on your time to make it worthwhile.

With that in mind, if you still want a master list, Rob Walch from Libsyn and the Podcast 411 show keeps a fairly up-to-date list at http://PaulColligan.com/RobsDirectory. Also popular is Daniel J. Lewis's "Podcast Places" (http://PaulColligan.com/PodcastPlaces).

The Dirty Little Secret About Podcast Directories

As cool as podcast directories are, they are for a very specific audience: people who like podcasts and want to know if there are additional shows that match their interests. This is a very small segment of the world, making directories a lousy place to put all your focus when building an audience.

You are not going to build any real audience just by being in a podcast directory — or all of them — even if you are uniquely positioned.

This might surprise you, but when Apple listed my show *The Podcast Report* (http://PaulColligan.com/ThePodcastReport) in a special "How To Podcast" section in iTunes, *it made no measurable difference to my audience size*. Think about it — what better promotion could my podcast get from them? I asked a few other podcasters on the list if they saw anything different and the answer was always "no." Does this mean iTunes is worthless? No. It just means that the iTunes audience is a small segment of the podcasting world, and not the only source for someone to build their audience. In short, podcast directories are a small piece of the podcast promotion process.

Where Do Listeners Come From?

Remember that old *Field of Dreams* movie with Kevin Costner, about the guy who hears a voice telling him to who built a baseball field on his Iowa farm? He kept hearing "If you build it, they will come." Well, this isn't the movies. Too many people now believe that "if you build it, they will come." In other words, if they launch their podcast, people will simply find them and listen or subscribe automatically. Nothing could be further from the truth. I've met too many people who simply don't understand why, now that their podcast is out, they don't have a huge listening audience instantly.

Sigh....

I'm going to be honest: the submission process I've listed here won't bring that much of an audience at all. It's better than nothing, sure, but it is your job to get the word out about your podcast. The rest of this chapter contains a few better ways to do that.

Start Building Your Audience with the Audience You Already Have

Let's start building a podcast audience with the people who already know, like and trust you. There is no better place to start a podcast audience than with them. You'd be surprised how many times I've had someone with a massive audience on another media ask me how to get the word out about their podcast. No matter how big or small your existing audience is, you need to tell them that you have a podcast and that they should check it out. Think about it — how else are they going to find out? It's not like they regularly log into iTunes and search to see if you are there.

In addition to telling them that you have a podcast, let them know: a) how to listen, and b) how to subscribe. When you tell them how to subscribe, make sure they know the benefits they get for doing so. If you don't know yourself, take a few minutes to figure that out. How do you do this? Any way possible. Email is best if you already have an email list. If you blog, tell them in a blog post.

However you currently communicate with your audience is the best way for you to tell them about your podcast. If you do voicemail or SMS blasts, send one out about your podcast. If you have a dry erase board at your place of business, make sure you write a message on it asking people to subscribe.I have one client who doubled their audience when they added a paper insert about their podcast to their monthly billing envelopes.

How can YOU best reach your audience with information about your show?

Enlisting Your Audience to Spread the Word

Once the people who know, like and trust you are listening to your podcast, you need to *ask them to share your show with others*. Give them a reason and the means to do so. This might seem odd to you at first, but you must realize that it will never happen if you don't ask.

This will result in one of two things: either they will share your show with others (and what better evangelist for your show than someone who already likes you?), or they won't. If they won't, you need to ask yourself (and them) why. If your show isn't worth telling others about, you need to change your show!

Don't know how to make your show worth sharing? Ask your audience. The people who are already listening are often more than willing to share their thoughts with you. If they're listening, plugging you into their earbuds or taking you with them on their morning commute, you have an intimacy with your audience that means you can ask for such feedback. Of course, don't put it all on them — make it easy to share your show. A Facebook page for your show is a great first step. You can see the one we've built for *The Podcast Report* at: http://PaulColligan.com/TPRFacebook.

Cross-Promotion

Another excellent way to build a podcast audience is by reaching out to *existing podcasts already catering to your audience*. Initially this may seem counterintuitive, but it works. It never hurts to approach other shows in your sphere to see if they'd be interested in cross-promoting.

You'll find most podcasters to be some of the most sharing and helpful people you'll ever meet. Reach out to them and see if there is a chance for some cross-promotion — you might be surprised at what they come up with.

Here's a little secret trick of podcast cross-promotion, so that you can get some exposure without having to ask for too much: reach out to a show you want to be highlighted on, and see if you can interview the host. The chances are good that they'll say yes — and of course, once the episode is released, chances are they will want to share it with their audience.

What Separates Your Podcast From All the Others is What Will Grow Your Audience More than Anything Else

Here's a little exercise that can do amazing things for you. Complete the following sentence:

The thing that separates my podcast from all the others in my genre is _____.

Once you figure that out, tell your audience. It's that simple.

An App For Your Podcast?

Another option for Podcast promotion is to create an individualized app specifically for your Podcast. This allows you to promote your show not just to the world of Podcast listeners, but to the much larger world of app users.

In late 2015, I launched an app for *The Podcast Report* that is free to download.

http://PaulColligan.com/TPRapp

Because I do a Podcast about Podcasting, I have little reason to promote the app version of my show and, as a result, only see small percentage of listeners from it. It's not a game-changer for me by any means but, it's nice to have this option. As you are well aware, the audience who uses apps is considerably bigger than the audience who listens to Podcasts. I'm thrilled to make my content available to both audiences.

One Last Promotion Opportunity

We've set up a Facebook page for this book at http://www.Facebook.com/HowToPodcast. When you publish your podcast, make sure to post it there — we'd all like to learn from you and be inspired by you. Hopefully, that might bring a little promotion to your show as well.

Tell the World

Hopefully I've started you along on the process of telling the world about your podcast. The podcast directories now know that you exist, so people looking for you there can find you.

Google has you indexed, which is great for common searches. You have alerted your audience and have started doing what you can to build from there.

Great job!

Step 4 Completed: NOW WHAT?

My goal for this book was always to show you how quickly and easily you can create a podcast. We've done that — but your journey has just begun.

Your Bonuses

I appreciate you trusting me with your time and money. I don't take it lightly.

My goal in books has always been to make the purchase a "no brainer" by offering a bunch of bonuses to anyone who picks up the book in either the digital or print edition. I hope to do the same with this version.

I"m not going to put an inflated value on these things - but, let's face it, they sure make the book worth your money.

If you register your copy of this book at http://HowToPodcastBook.com I'll send you an email with the following;

A coupon for $100 off my How To Podcast online training program. If you need a deeper look into the process examined here (or are just one of those types who learns better by video), you can now get in a much less than the public can.

A batch of high resolution PDFs of all of the graphics in this book. Want a few pieces of inspiration to put on your walls? You got 'em.

A video series where I went over the four steps and how they were used to create an episode of *The Podcast Report*. It's a view from my desktop and may help answer any questions you might have.

Sign up before my live webinar "What's changed in Podcasting and how you can profit from it?" happens, and you get a free ticket to the live event. Register afterwards and I'll make sure you get the recording.

Previous versions of this book included over 100 pages of commentary and training about the Podcast space from some of my favorite people in the industry. I'll send you the digital version of this content for the ereader of your choice - yes it will work on Kindle, iBooks, and I'll even send a PDF version.

There will be some other cool bonuses and offers that I won't list here ...

In the interest of full disclosure, everyone who registers the book will get occasional emails from me, including my *Heads Up Tuesday* email newsletter where I give you the highlights of what you need to know in online media each week. You'll be able to unsubscribe at any time.

In addition, if something changes drastically in the world of podcasting, and you're still on the list, I'll send you an update and keep you in the know.

So, register the book at http://HowToPodcastBook.com and I'll get these and a few other bonuses, right out to you.

What's Next?

You now know how to podcast. You're also probably pretty surprised at how easy it is if you've made it this far in the book.

You have everything you need - and those great bonuses too - if you registered the book!

Honestly, nothing would thrill me more than to have you simply close this book, record your first podcast, get it live and post your success story on our Facebook page.

http://www.Facebook.com/HowToPodcast

Thanks for coming along on this journey with me.

In reality, the journey to podcast success is a bit more than just creating a podcast and making it available to the world. Once you are live, you still need to use it to expand your reach to as many people as is possible and leverage the tech of this exciting platform to build your business.

Following this chapter are three bonus chapters. First is a simple piece called *What To Know Before You Start Podcasting*. The goal of these few pages is to help you understand a few things about starting a podcasting that aren't about the technical bits we examined earlier in this book.

That chapter is followed by the transcripts from two interviews from *The Podcast Report* with two of my favorite podcasters: John Lee Dumas and Russell Brunson. John Lee shares some of his amazing rapid content creation techniques. The amount of content John Lee produces is incredible. He has more than sixteen hundred episodes so far. Russell Brunson will both surprise you with his technology choices and inspire you with his marketing strategy. They're both great guys, great podcasters and have really leveraged the industry to create some impressive profits. I've learned a lot from them and I know you can to.

Even though there is so much in this one book, there are a number of ideas and tips that t couldn't fit in. Make sure you register your book at http://www.HowToPodcastBook.com to get it all. When you sign up, I will also email you my weekly *Heads Up Tuesday* newsletter so you'll stay up to date on the latest in podcasting. Of course, you can unsubscribe at any time.

Finally, at the time of writing, I have more than 125 episodes recorded of *The Podcast Report* over at http://ThePodcastReport.com. If you interested in more of the business of podcasting, please visit and subscribe to the show.

I close by asking a simple question:

When will you record your first episode and how will you let the world know?

Paul Colligan

Portland, Oregon

Expand Reach - Leverage Tech

What To Know Before You Start Podcasting

Now that you know the details of Podcasting and the mechanics of getting one out the door, I wanted to take just a few pages to give you insight into some of the challenges that you might come up against in your first days of this exciting venture.

The old axiom "failing to plan is planning to fail" is as true in Podcasting as it is anywhere else. Having helped readers, students and Podcast Partnership clients launch Podcasts for over a decade now, I have the unique perspective of seeing what works and what doesn't. Too many podcasts start with enthusiasm for what's possible yet die in a whimper of what wasn't expected. There is no need for that to happen to you.

Here are the most important things you need to know before you start podcasting:

Your first podcast will be your worst podcast

NOBODY sounds they way they want to sound on their first episode. You can respond to this reality in two different ways: 1) spend the rest of your life massaging your podcast so that you can release the perfect first episode or 2) get that first episode out the door as quickly as possible and know that you will only be going up from there.

The money doesn't come in without a plan

If you are hoping to see a revenue stream from your show, you better have a strategy for making it happen. The idea that you'll one day pick up sponsors is, simply, the worst possible approach with the lowest chances of success. A plan for monetization, even an imperfect one, will always bring better results and more cash than no plan. It might change a thousand times before you see your first check but, at the very least, have a plan going into this.

Perfection is the enemy of the podcast

No podcast is ever perfect. Trying for perfection will get in the way of getting out your content - the very reason you started podcasting in the first place. Yes, you should make your podcast sound as good as it possibly can, but make getting your message out the priority.

Go for impact, not just downloads

Most wouldn't consider a podcast with a single download per episode a great success... unless the one download was by the President of the United States. I can't promise you the President for an audience, but I can tell you that if you focus on impact over downloads, you'll have a much better show in the end.

Always consider Apple

You may have started your podcast because you're a big fan of Apple, or you may be the podcaster without an Apple device of their own. Regardless of your opinion, the fact is that the average Podcast has an audience of sixty to eighty percent Apple users, so you better make sure your presentation looks good on Apple devices and in the iTunes software. ITunes is free to download, even without an iOS device, so be sure to check everything you do against it.

You are responsible for your marketing

Podcasting is not an "if you build it, they will come" venture. Despite, what you've heard, being in the directories has never built a real audience. Just like no business would ever have been successful with only their name listed in the phonebook white pages, you need more than a directory listing to reach your audience Work out your marketing strategy before you record that first episode.

Consider the source

Opinions are plentiful in the podcasting space. When you hear something about podcasting, consider the source of the opinion and ask a few questions: Does the person have a podcast? How long have they been podcasting? Are they seeing success in the topic they have opinions about? Are they giving "professional" advice, yet have a different day job? You wouldn't take weight loss advice from a 400 pound man and I'm sure you wouldn't trust your investments to a five year old child. Always consider the source.

Bonus: Answer These Questions To Do Real Business With Your Podcast

Although it was never my intention to make this book about the business of podcasting, I want to make sure anyone reading this is, at the very least, is pointed in the right direction. The following worksheet asks four simple questions. Answer these before you launch a business podcast.

TO DO REAL BUSINESS WITH YOUR PODCAST

ANSWER THESE 7 QUESTIONS:

1) Market Match: Does your target audience match your market?:

Who is your audience? You must be able to describe your audience avatar. What do they want from your podcast and how you are going to deliver it to them? Don't go any further until you have a clear answer.

2) Message Match: Does your message match your market's needs? :

What message are you communicating to your your audience? Find your message match by completing this sentence:

This is the show where we help _____ to _____ so that they can _____.

3) Money Match: How will your message generate revenue for your business? :

The question is obvious. The answer isn't always clear. Don't progress with your show until you have a specific strategy.

4) Media Match: Is podcasting an effective way to reach your audience?

Does your audience listen to podcasts? Could you serve them better on another media platform like live streaming, social video, or even print? Podcasting isn't the answer to everything.

5) Production Machine: How are you going to produce your podcast?

Since there is no money in production itself, how are you going to produce your podcast with as little friction, and as quickly, as possible? An inefficient production process can end up costing valuable resources of money and time - and prevent you from getting your message out.

6) Marketing Machine: How will your audience find you?

Once your Podcast is ready to share with the world, how will your audience find you? Tip - just being listed in the directories won't be enough to generate real business.

7) Tracking Machine: How will you know if your podcast is working?

If you can't track success, you'll never know if you have it or not. What factors do you want to track and how will you stay informed? "Failing to plan is planning to fail." It's ok to change tactics as your podcast develops, but you need to start out with a plan.

WARNING: DON'T LAUNCH YOUR PODCAST UNTIL YOU HAVE A PLAN FOR THESE 7 THINGS

HowToPodcastBook.com • HowToPodcastTraining.com

John Lee Dumas on Making Media

*The following is a transcript from Episode #30 of **The Podcast Report** (http://PaulColligan..com/ThePodcastReport) where I interviewed John Lee Dumas of **Entrepreneur On Fire** (http://PaulColligan.com/EntrpreneurOnFire) about his strategies for Rapid Content Production. John is a MACHINE when it comes to content creation. He does a show every day of the week, and I want to have him share about his methods.*

Paul Colligan:

I'm on the Skype line with John Lee Dumas, *Entrepreneur on Fire*. Sir, you've said it so many times. *Are you ready to... ignite?*

John Lee Dumas:

Paul, let's set this place on fire.

Paul Colligan:

Let's do it my friend. I am impressed with what you've done and it's funny, because some of the things I'm impressed with are not the same things which others are impressed with. Maybe that means I've got bad focus... but hey, it's my show - so let's get to work here. The first thing is: you produce a considerable amount of content.

I've been on your show. You sent me the questionnaire. You ask the same questions to everybody. Everybody is familiar with the questions; they like the questions; they're familiar. How much additional time do you spend on your show producing content other than the interviews that you do?

John Lee Dumas:

Not much, is the answer. What we have set up is really a system that does flow just like you shared. We have our studio days, which are just Tuesdays with eight back-to-back interviews. By 6 p.m. that night, I not only have interviewed eight people, but it is edited, it is produced and it is (for the most part) uploaded and ready to go on that one day. From that point, it's all my virtual assistants; they take over. They're the ones who set up the processes, the follow-ups, the marketing of it in the social media which keeps the machine going. It really was a system that I set up at a large cost and with a lot of time - once. Now it just works for me.

Paul Colligan:

A 40-minute show takes you 40 minutes to make?

John Lee Dumas:

I'd say a 40-minute show takes me 50 minutes to make. That's because I do drop markers throughout the interviews; for example, if there's a swear word or something a little excessive. I might go in and splice that out - but it's super minimal. I'd say I spend no more than 5-10 minutes on that per show.

Paul Colligan:

Awesome. This is something which I think gets missed. Now, you mentioned the batching and a lot of people know about it, but there are like three people left on the planet who still don't know about you, my friend. You said that you tape all of your shows on Tuesday, did I hear that right? This is obviously a leading question: you do eight interviews on Tuesday?

John Lee Dumas:

Yes. First off, I hope those three people who have not heard about me are listening to you, Paul. Starting at 9 a.m. every Tuesday, I do an interview on the hour, every single hour, until 4 p.m. That's when my last interview starts. By the time 5 p.m. rolls around, I have eight interviews complete. By the time 6 p.m. hits, I've edited those at an average rate of five minutes a clip for all eight - and I'm done for that week, plus one day of interviews. As we sit here right now, I'm actually booked out every single Tuesday for the next three-and-a-half months. I know that Tuesday is a full studio day.

Paul Colligan:

That's one day, and I won't say one fifth of your week because I know you work like a mad man, but...

John Lee Dumas:

One seventh.

Paul Colligan:

One eight-hour session and all the shows are done.

John Lee Dumas:

Done.

Paul Colligan:

Does that exhaust you? How do you have the energy to do that? Talk to me.

John Lee Dumas:

I do equate it a little bit to training for a marathon. I'm not a great runner. I do jog every now and then but after two miles I'm done, put a fork in me... and that's pretty much it. However, I have trained for half marathons and marathons before and I could never run either one of those right now - but I could train and then eventually be able to run one.

When I first started **Entrepreneur on Fire**, Paul, I was doing three or four interviews a day, two or three days a week. I was toast at the end of those days. I saw how much time it took me to set up for each one, then to break down for each one. It was becoming my week. So, that's when I decided to draw a line in the sand and say, "It's got to be one day and basically, I've got to build up the energy for this." Just like you can build up running energy, I wanted to build up interviewing energy. It hasn't come easy. It's definitely been a process, and with every single month that has gone by, it has become a little bit easier. But there were times that at the end, I felt near to collapsing or saying, "Okay, I need some spaghetti. I need a blanket. That's it - no more." Now, honestly, I can do eight interviews and be like, "Alright, what's next? Let's do a live webinar." It's gotten to that point; but it did take a while and it was a process to get here.

Paul Colligan:

Would it be easier to do two sets of four interviews, take two half days or something like that?

John Lee Dumas:

I think it would have been when I started. That's probably where I should have stayed longer to be honest, because it would have resulted in higher quality interviews. Back in the 300s and 400s of my interview episodes, back when it really still was a strain for me, by episode six, seven and eight, I was flagging mentally. It was just kind of hard to conjure up that same type of energy. It's pretty funny; I just interviewed somebody for episode 872. I also interviewed her for episode 61. I went back and just listened to a couple of minutes of that first interview right before I kicked into our second interview. I was like, "Wow!" I was uninspiring; I was so flat. I had no energy in that interview compared to what I have now. That came with feeling more comfortable and doing it more often; also, she was probably episode seven or eight of the day on the first interview, and I was just flagging at that point.

But to be honest with you, now, I look forward to each interview of the eight. I get really fired up just getting into these conversations. I'm at the point where I love my eight-interview days. Firstly, because I can do it without breaking sweat. Secondly, because it doesn't take up blocks of my other days where I'm doing other things: creating courses, writing books, doing all the cool things that need to be done.

Paul Colligan:

That's good. That's good. Now, again, for those three people who haven't heard of you, every episode of your show follows a format. You send the interviewee a batch of questions. You ask the questions and you do it. It's brilliant, because it makes it easier for you and you don't have to do a tremendous amount of research. I was listening to an interview with Tony Robbins and he said he does 18 hours of research before he meets with somebody. I was like, "Oh my goodness." You don't have to do any research and you could probably do all the questions by heart now. I imagine that for your first 500 shows, you had a cheat sheet. After that, it's probably just second nature to you.

What I found interesting is that there are a lot of podcasters, unfortunately, who have decided that if they just have a batch of questions and if they just do eight a week, they'll see the same success that you've had. It's a bad concept and it's a bad idea; largely just because this is is the formula that works for you. This is the model that works for you. This is what makes your nature happen. It wasn't that you stumbled across this. You did a heck of a lot of work, a heck of a lot planning, a heck of a lot of strategy before all this happened and said, "Hey, this is a formula that makes sense to John." What would you say to somebody who's trying to create content, trying to come up with a formula that makes sense to Fred or to Becky or to Frank?

John Lee Dumas:

I love the question - and before I answer, I just want to go back and reiterate how correct you are on the initial point that you made, which is that when I wake up on Tuesday morning, I don't even know who the eight people are that I'm going to be interviewing. That's because I haven't yet opened up my spreadsheet that my VA creates and she updates. It's literally sometimes only ten minutes before my interview starts when I'll pull it up and say, "Okay here's my eight people. Oh, I know. I know that person and that person a little bit. I've heard of that person." I don't have to know who I'm going to be interviewing, because of the system I've set up; it doesn't require me to know anything before the interview starts, because I have those formatted questions.

In a way, I like not knowing too much because it makes me curious and it makes me, in my opinion, ask the questions to follow up their answers that I would want, that I hope and want my listeners on Fire Nation to be asking. That's just kind of a little reiteration on a point that you made that I definitely want to second. It's huge for me because it just takes away so much mental bandwidth - like what you mentioned with Tony Robbins. I can't do 18 hours of prep! I don't even take 18 minutes for eight interviews to prep, I don't. It's just all right there. All I know is their 50-word intro that I'm reading over once right before I introduce them, when I usually have them on Skype already.

To answer your last question, for someone who's listening right now and they're saying, "I want to create something, but how do I know what the right frequency is? How do I know what the right content is? How do I know this, how do I know that?" I created **Entrepreneur on Fire** because it was what I wanted. I was so tired of listening to a great podcast episode with an inspiring entrepreneur, getting so much out of it and then knowing that I have to wait two more weeks, or another week for that next interview. I also hated those interviews where people were going on and on about cats, or maybe they're talking about sports one day, but they weren't quite getting to the meat. I thought, "To me, the perfect podcast would be seven days a week." I knew that if I press the play button, I was going to hear what I wanted to hear. That I was going to hear an actual journey from a successful entrepreneur who is going to be sharing their failures, their lessons learned, their "Aha!" moments, their success.

I thought, "I want that. I want to give that to Fire Nation." Boom - **Entrepreneur on Fire** was born. That was how my show came about. If you're listening right now, that's how your show needs to come about. You need to really get angry or frustrated or depressed because the show you want to listen to doesn't exist. When you know what that show is, then you go out and give birth to it and create it. That's going to ensure that you're drawing people in and that the audience is going to resonate with you as a host and your content as a whole.

Paul Colligan:

There are two things I love about you, John... well, there are a lot, but we're just going to list two for now. Firstly, you have a crystal clear understanding of who your avatar is. You've said that from day one, "I am the avatar. I'm making the show the I want to listen to." Now, not everybody has that opportunity, not everybody has that gift, for lack of a better term, but you're crystal clear about it. That's what anybody can take away from this.

Secondly, the thing that I really love is that the secret to your success - one of the many secrets to your success - is not the formula. It's not the excitement. It's not the "fire" part of it. It is the fact that you have such a close and intimate relationship with your avatar. You know exactly who you're creating for. There is no doubt why your podcast is and what your podcast is in your mind.

That clarity is phenomenal. That clarity is worth a million bucks. What would you say to people struggling to figure out their avatar? Or spending too much time on content creation and editing because they're not quite sure what they want? Maybe we don't have the intimacy that John has with his avatar, but how can we get that kind of intimacy?

John Lee Dumas:

Avatar is everything, in my opinion, when it comes to creating a podcast. I think one thing that a lot of people do miss is that they think about what their avatar has to be in some way, in broad shapes and forms. I say that because every time I speak in a conference or I'm talking and I get asked this question on someone else's podcast, then I always turn the question around and I say, "Who out there has a podcast? Okay raise your hand. Okay, how long have you been podcasting? Oh, you have 100 episodes a year. You must know who your one perfect listener is, who that avatar is. Stand up and share with the world."

Sure enough, they'll puff their chest out and they'll stand up and they'll say, "My avatar is males between ages 25 and 45 who like to drink coffee and watch football on the weekends." I'm like, that's barely a targeted demographic. That is not an avatar; you don't know who your avatar is. I've given my avatar spiel a lot. My avatar is Jimmy. He is identical to who I was when I launched *Entrepreneur on Fire.*

I know exactly who that person is. Whenever I come to a fork in the road, I don't make that decision; it's not my bandwidth, it's Jimmy's bandwidth, because he knows, left or right, straight off the bat. If you're listening right now, you're saying, "I'm struggling to create my avatar because I want so many people to listen. I want to grow a large audience." Remember, if you try to resonate with everybody and make a vague avatar to resonate with everybody, you're going to resonate with nobody. You need to be one of these people who says, "You know what, I know exactly one person who would be perfect to listen to my podcast, and I'm going to create my podcast for that person." Get a niche in there.

Actually, just get a handhold and start building a little momentum. Then start having that momentum work outwards. You can expand the scope outwards from that point and grow a bigger show; you can go from niching down to bringing it back out. Just go out and grow a bigger audience. But so many of us, Paul, are afraid to start small. Because we think if we start small, we'll always be small. But the problem is, we have to start small to get big. If we start big, we'll never even get going because we'll just get lost in this ocean. I've seen it time and time again. There's over 1,900 people in **Podcaster's Paradise**. I watch their launches and I watch their trajectory.

Those that are still crushing it six, twelve or eighteen months later, are those that just say, "You know what? This is the perfect listener. I'm going to podcast to that person until I've dominated that niche. Then I'm going to take one step back out. Then I'm going to build this larger audience as I continue to move outwards." Those are the people who have found success. Don't be afraid to get specific, to start really focused in and just be that avatar if it's you, or create that avatar if it's somebody else.

Paul Colligan:

Who do you think is doing this, and you probably know a lot of them, especially with 1,900 right now in **Podcaster's Paradise** (http://PaulColligan.com/Paradise), you said?

John Lee Dumas:

Yes.

Paul Colligan:

You probably know a lot of them. Pick someone that maybe we'd have a better chance than others to recognize. Who else out there do you think really understands their avatar?

John Lee Dumas:

I would actually just like to poll up our Facebook group, because it's so cool to see these discussions and these hangouts that we do and how focused the actual word "avatar" is in my community (**Paradise** - (http://PaulColligan.com/Paradise). To see these people going back and forth, saying, "That's not niche enough. That's not focused enough." But one person who I love talking about is Paul Blaise. He has a podcast called **Potters Cast**. It's about making pots. It's handcrafted pots.

Picture the movie *Ghost*, Paul. Paul Blaise is like that; it's a podcast for people who actually make pots like in the movie *Ghost*; handcrafted pots. His podcast is so specific, so focused. If he gets 600 listens per episode, it's a good day. In fact, it's a great day, because 600 people who are listening to a podcast about how to make pottery, hand-thrown pottery, is a massive audience for that niche. He knows that exact avatar. He knows the age of that person. He knows where that person is going; he knows they are going to their local college at night to take the courses.

He knows how he can reach out to colleges and have them mention his podcast during their courses. He brings in those teachers, who actually teach these college communication courses at these state universities and community colleges around the country, onto his show. They share it with their students... and then it starts to spread like wildfire within the community. That's an example of a guy who does a podcast about making pots. He's having a great time doing it, because it's his passion and he's very successful with it.

Paul Colligan:

Beautiful. I will get that in the show notes and in the transcript. We'll get a link for that to happen as well. I'm going to want to close this up, but I'm going to be respectful of your time. Do you have any final words? Part one of the book is "Make Digital Media". That's the first step, and you just started making media like a racehorse out the traps. I love that, because I've met people (and I'm sure I said that you probably met them too) who six months later have yet to hit the record button. What would you say to someone who's just a deer in the headlights when it comes to making media, and has yet to hit that red button? What would you say to them, John?

John Lee Dumas:

Paul, I love this. I love to make media. One of my favorite quotes, which ties right in with this and really just underscores this and helped me to get this far, is: "If you want to be, do." I wanted to be a podcaster, Paul. I had zero experience; I had zero online presence; I'd never spoken into a microphone before or interviewed anybody... but I wanted to be a podcaster. The only way that I was going to be a podcaster was by doing that thing, was by podcasting.

I was willing to have the courage to be bad, because it does take that courage. For a decent amount of time, slowly getting better by practicing the craft, by pressing that red button every single day, talking to somebody that was so much more successful, so much more eloquent, so much more polished, so much more impressive than me; bumbling around, acting the fool, stumbling over my words, trying to have a coherent conversation.

But every time I'd think: "Wow, that was bad, but I did a little bit better on this or on that." I'm just doing that every single day and now I'm at episode 835. That is the reality of just doing; that's why I love making media. I would ask them, "What are you doing? I don't want to hear any excuses. You're about to say 10 reasons why you're not making media? Make media." That's all that matters and that's why I love that message.

Paul Colligan:

Do we have an attribution for "If you want to be, do," or does that come from you?

John Lee Dumas:

I've Googled it over and over; I've looked everywhere. Brainy Quotes seems to have everything, but right now I just can't find out who to attribute that quote to. I'm tempted to take it... but I know that I've heard it from somewhere else.

Paul Colligan:

Very cool John. Thank you so much, man. It's about making media. You do it with an enthusiasm and, dare I say, a fire that I see nobody else doing it with. You do it with a great amount of strategy and understanding and empathy towards your avatar, which gets the results. It's a great formula, I'm glad you're doing it, I love the show. But it's your understanding of what you are doing which produced this formula, and I think that is such a testimony to what you've got there. Thank you so much for the interview, man. I want to be good to your time. Thanks.

John Lee Dumas:

Paul, with those words, I can die happy, my friend. Thank you kindly.

Paul Colligan:

There it is, John in all his glory. I love this guy. I love what he's doing, I love what he's done, I love the model that he's created. I'm thrilled to share him with you, *The Podcast Report* audience.

Russell Brunson Is Marketing In His Car

I'd like to take this next chapter and share with you the podcast success story of my good friend, Russell Brunson. Russell is a genius at marketing, and he came up with one of the most innovative and successful podcasts I've seen in all the years I've been podcasting.

Russell records his Podcast using nothing but his phone. His marketing model keeps him at the top of the charts and generates real money.

Bottom line: He buys his audience with his marketing model.

How is this possible?

Read on and see exactly how he does it.

Here's the link to the original episode of the Podcast where I interview Russell:
http://PaulColligan.com/RussellOnPodcast

Here's a link to Russell's show: (Note, he recently changed the name - same show though.)

http://PaulColligan.com/RussellsShow

Here's a link to Russell's "free" MP3 player offer:

http://PaulColligan.com/RussellsMP3Offer

Here's a link to Russell's Podcast Funnel at ClickFunnels:

http://PaulColligan.com/PodcastClickFunnel

Russell started out simply recording what he was learning and thinking about in marketing in his car during his commute to work. That's all he did. No script, no fancy equipment, just Russell and his ideas, recorded in his car on his cell phone, podcast directly to his audience. It was raw, real, unfiltered, and fantastic.

His podcast, *Marketing In Your Car*, went on for several years and has been a solid audience builder and profit maker. I checked in on Russell recently, and low and behold, Russell's podcast was going up the charts in the management and marketing categories. Read on to hear my interview with Russell and learn the creative strategy that has propelled his podcast to success.

Paul Colligan:

Today I've got Russell Brunson on the Skype phone. Russell, how are you doing buddy?

Russell Brunson:

I'm doing awesome man, how have you been?

Paul Colligan:

I'm doing well. Now you work harder, faster, deeper than anyone else I know. You're killing it with Click Funnels. You're killing it with all of the things that you're doing. You actually started a podcast a little while ago. Why did you start a podcast, other than I prodded you into it?

Russell Brunson:

What's funny is you did prod, like ten years ago, whenever podcasting became a word and I just didn't understand it. That's when we started hanging out. You kept saying, "You gotta do a podcast." And if you remember, I actually had one of your friends write the theme song for the first podcast like ten years ago, but I never actually did the podcast because I had no time, right? And then man, it was probably about three years ago now and it was on the back end of one of my big businesses collapsing and imploding, and I was kind of restarting over from scratch. And I thought, you know, I just want to do this podcasting thing. I have no idea if it's going to work, or how it's going to work. But I just want to start doing it. And what's interesting is, I tried to figure out a format in a way that I would be consistent and actually do it. It really started out as a therapeutic thing for me to start talking about what was happening and what we were going through and like the wins we were having and the loss we were having, and kind of just daily talking about what was happening in my life. That's where it all started, and it's become part of my day now. I really enjoy it. I'm checking in with my people and sharing the cool stuff and working behind the scenes and it's become part of what we do now. But it definitely started as just you prodding me, me taking five or six years and then finally just jumping in and doing it, and then kind of becoming addicted to it.

Paul Colligan:

Now how many episodes are you into it?

Russell Brunson:

We are almost to our 300th episode. I think it's 296 I record this morning. So it's pretty crazy actually when you think about it.

Paul Colligan:

So here you are, you know, Mr. Internet Wonderkid, Mr. Internet Millionaire, Mr. Internet Fancy Pants, hanging out with Tony Robbins kind of guy. And you don't even spend money on a microphone. I mean you're podcasting from your cell phone on the way into work. Why didn't you buy a better microphone?

Russell Brunson:

You know, it cracks me up. I get people, man probably four or five times a week who message me from all sorts of places, that they love my podcast and asking "So how do I do it? What's the microphone you're using? The audio sounds so good and so clear, " and all these things. And I always laugh because yeah, in fact when we first started I bought one of those little mics you plug into an iPhone and then you hook it to your shirt and you can talk in it. But the problem with that is like 99% of the time I forget the thing, I forget the microphone, and then I decided I was going to podcast. I have this really cool idea and I'm like, "Oh wait, I don't have a microphone! Oh okay, I'll do it tomorrow." Then I forgot the microphone. And it just killed all of the spontaneity around it and it became this huge hurdle that stopped me from actually doing it. I thought, "You know what, I need to create this in a way that fits in my lifestyle so I can do a podcast anywhere, at anytime without having to think about equipment." As long as my phone is in my hand, I can share my thoughts in the moment. I don't know about you, but when you have an idea, right, and you script it out and you share it with people two or three weeks later, you lose the passion of the moment. And for me it's like when I share something, it's usually in the beginning before it's about to happen or right after something bad has happened, and I'm emotionally charged right now. This is the time I want to share it with my audience. I won't have time to find a microphone or anything, I just want to be able to talk. So I think what we may lose in quality by using just the internal phone on my iPhone, I think we gain in being in the moment and being present and being being engaged in that level. For me that's kind of why I do it, and it doesn't give me an out. It forces me when I'm ready or when something happens to share it right then and I think that's why people connect with the podcast is because that's how it's happening. It's happening live. It's not scripted or thought through at all. I click record and then I go.

Paul Colligan:

But it's just a passion project, right? You're not making any money from recording from a phone?

Russell Brunson:

So initially I think it was and the cool thing is I didn't know. I should have called you. It was one of those ego things. I was thinking I know a lot so I didn't reach out to my friends who are really smart on stuff. So I just launched the podcast and I didn't know how to set it up. I had no tracking, I had no stats. And it's funny because we, literally two weeks ago, finally got the tracking steps and I finally know how many people are listening. But prior to that, like I had no idea. And I'm actually so grateful I did because if I had known that nobody was listening for the first year and a half, I probably would have stopped. But I had no idea. I just thought "Well maybe there are people that like this?" So I kept doing it and doing it. But what's interesting, and the reason why it's becoming more and more of a focus for me, is a couple of years ago I launched what I call my "Inner Circle." It's my high end clients and people that pay $25,000 a year to be in it. It's interesting; as we grew from a couple people to ten to thirty, now we have 100 people and capped it at that. There is one really, really interesting common thread between my inner circle members: almost all of them were podcast listeners. I was like, "How weird is that?" The people that have become my best customers are all people who had me in their ear and have listened over and over and over. It's like they know me at a different, more intimate level.

They are the ones who trust me at this level of my business. So while it definitely began as a fun thing, I mean, I can directly attribute millions of dollars a year to the podcast. I don't think my podcast had a call to action until episode like 200 and something - and the call to action was like go get the free MP3 player with more episodes - it was never something that was designed and choreographed to sell and set things up. It was just me sharing the struggles that I had as an entrepreneur and connecting with people at that level. And what's crazy about that is when you do it and you are completely vulnerable... I mean, I had episodes where I shared stuff I don't think my wife knows about me, but I just share it because it's important for entrepreneurs to see. Not just the ups that everyone likes to brag about, but I want people to see the downs and the frustrations and the times that I've wanted to quit. I share those things because it's real. I think because of that it builds a different level of connection, and like I said, my best clients tell me, "Russell, I'm addicted to your podcast, that's why I'm in your inner circle." That's such a weird thing. It wasn't because of a good sales video, or a good sales letter, or a webinar that hooked them or the sales process. It was that I was communicating with them on a very personal level that they related with and that build trust and relationship with me.

That's why they've ascended up and become our best clients. So it definitely started out as just a thing, but it's morphed into something. In fact, and we're going to talk about this a little bit, this big relaunch that we're doing about the podcast. I look at this common thread of all my best clients listening to me daily in their ears, so I want to take all the rest of my clients and get them doing that. Because if they do, then hopefully they will become my best clients as well. They will ascend up the same way those other people did. And so yeah, it's definitely become crazy profitable for us now, but it wasn't probably for the first year, year and half. I mean I don't even know when because we didn't track it. But looking back on it now, it's probably one of the best things we've ever done for our business.

Paul Colligan:

Now Russell. I'm doing some math here. Okay: The average podcast sells ads and the average ad rate is 40 CPM. And that 40 CPM that means 40 bucks per thousand downloads. So you are saying it's easier to get somebody into a $25,000 mastermind than it is to get 625,000 people to download your show?

Russell Brunson:

Yes. Holy cow yes. And I always think about this: If somebody is willing to pay me that much to be in front of my audience, I should be able to make a lot more than that just by being awesome. People always ask me, "Can I buy ads in your thing?" I'm like, "No because you could monetize better than me." Then I've got to become a better marketer. I've got to figure out how to do that. So I think it's a million times easier.

Paul Colligan:

So it's easier to get somebody to pay you $25,000 than it is to get 625,000 downloads?

Russell Brunson:

By far.

Paul Colligan:

And on a microphone that's just your phone. I mean you couldn't even, I mean here these people are paying you all this money, aren't they worthy of a good microphone?

Russell Brunson:

There is a double edged sword there. They are definitely worthy of that. But again the problem is I think most of us are so concerned about that face that we share with the world, because we want to look good. That's what keeps people from connecting with you. You know what I mean? It's almost like when we put away those things and just connect at a personal level, that's when a real connection happens. And in today's world, that's what we want, that's what all of us are striving for - the relationships. The reason why we buy what we do, we connect with people the way we do is because there is that connection. And I think that yeah you lose that sometimes with being too polished. I think it's about sharing the truth and the truth is what draws people to you.

Paul Colligan:

So you did this for a while. And you moved over to some new stats. And you got some realizations. You had your moment when you realized your best customer consumes your podcast, and by the way, that's not a weird thread, I get that from everyone. And then, you decided to give away MP3 players driving people to listen to your show. Now this is not a topic that you normally read in the *How To Get More Listeners* books that you can get over at Amazon. Why are you giving, and let's be honest, it's a $9.95 shipping and handling, for those of you who can get an MP3 player delivered to your house for $9.95, please let us both know. But the fact of the matter is you are giving away an MP3 player to get more listeners to your show. What the heck is that about?

Russell Brunson:

Yeah, so there is a backstory to this. So what happened is we started seeing the podcast results from this as like "Dang this is cool, how do we grow it?" Well, just keep doing your show and people will organically come to you. But I'm not patient. I'm like, okay, that's nice, but I want, I don't know how many listeners I have at this point, maybe a hundred, maybe a thousand, maybe five thousand, I don't know, but I want more of them. So let's give them more. So for me I'm looking at let's go to Facebook and let's buy ads. And so we started buying ads. Everyone who has a good podcast, right, we are buying ads directly to their audiences, right? I'm like "Hey, they listen to *Entrepreneur on Fire*, they should listen to mine. They are listening to Paul's Podcast, they should listen to mine. So we are looking at all these things. And so I have my, guy on my team that does all of our ads, I start having him spend money on Facebook ads to drive people to subscribe to our podcast. And so he's spending a whole bunch of money. I mean a thousand bucks a day or so. It's kind of like the budget. Things are happening and it's running for a week or two and I'm like "Cool! How many subscribers, how much are we paying per subscriber? How is it all working?" And he said, "I don't know." I said "What do you mean you don't know?" He's said "I can't track if they actually subscribe to iTunes or what's happening. There is no way I can track. I can dump money into it and we can cross our fingers and hope, but there is no way…

95

Well maybe there is, but we didn't know a way to actually tell that." So I said, "Okay, so we're just throwing money in and hoping something happens and we have no idea?" I mean that goes against everything I believe in in advertising. I want to be able to track everything I do. So I told him just stop. So for a week or two I was frustrated. I was thinking "How do we stimulate the growth of this podcast?" I can't do it. And then one day I was driving, and actually I did a whole podcast on this before. I was like, "I have an idea. I think I figured out how I can actually pay to build my podcast, and pay in a way that's predictable and doesn't actually cost me any money!" So I did a podcast, probably about ten episodes, 15 episodes ago or something like that, and I shared the strategy of what I was going to try to do, and we went and did it and it's been awesome. So basically the strategy was I need a hook that would be interesting for people. So I thought, "The podcast is free right now, so I can't sell the podcast. How do I make this so people will actually pay for it? What if we took a bunch of episodes and put them on a pre-loaded MP3 player? That's kind of a cool idea." And so we connected with people in China and we had them build a really cool MP3 player, put it in a cool box and preloaded the first 257 episodes and so now I had a hook. I could go and I could advertise to people that had big podcast followings and say, "Hey if you like marketing podcasts, go get a free MP3 player at marketingcar.com." and it would actually pay.

Now I could start seeing what's happening. If I spend a dollar on Facebook ads, like what's going to happen? So what happens is we started driving people to the free MP3 player and again they pay shipping and handling, so there is a little bit of a cost. They put their credit card in, and on the page, if you guys go through this process you'll see it, we took the transcripts of those first 257 episodes as well. We put them in a PDF, because my audience, tons of them like to read as well. So I said for an extra $17, I'll give you the PDF. It's 1,000 pages. I think it ended up being of all the transcripts of marketing in your car of the first 257 episodes. You can read it on your Kindle or on your phone or whatever it is. That way you could read along as well. If I could find the numbers real quick. From that, let's see my team sent me an update yesterday I believe. So let me see if I can find it real quick. Sheer numbers...

Paul Colligan:

So while you are looking at this, people go to the page and you say free MP3 player, shipping and handling $9.95 and by the way if you go to ThePodcastReport.com/115, we'll have a link to this whole process and a link to Russell's episode where he came up with this as well. You pay the $9.95 for the MP3 player and on the next page it says, "Would you like to pay $17 for the transcripts?"

Russell Brunson:

So this same page is something we call on our Clickfunnels world, an order form bump. So they put in their credit card and right before the submit button there is a little paragraph that says, "Hey would you also like the transcripts for an extra $17 dollars?" So right now 29.7% of the people who ordered the free MP3 player upgrade also get the transcripts. So one out of three. Almost one out of three are paying an extra $17 to get the transcripts. So all of a sudden, now I can spend money on Facebook ads and I can recoup that money and I just added a subscriber. Honestly, what happens right now is for every MP3 that we're giving away, I don't know the exact number, but we're getting multiple people to subscribe to the podcast, o that's kind of the first step. Now after that we have an upsell for our membership site, and from that 17.9% of people are joining my membership site, which for us is $67 a month. So that's pretty crazy. Then after that we have a $300 offer which is a bunch of our trainings and we are getting about 4.6% of people take that. So the metrics that I look at in my business, I'm from the funnel world, so we have a couple metrics that drive everything we do. The first thing is to find what our cost is to acquire a customer. So how much does it cost me to get somebody this free MP3 player? And right now we are averaging a $15 cost in Facebook ads to get somebody to buy the MP3 player. But then the second metrics is called our average cart value. So for everyone who buys the MP3 player, on average how much money do we make when they go through that sales funnel immediately? And so before any of the continuity kicks in, our average cart value right now in this funnel is $32.12. So that means I'm spending $15 to give away an MP3 player and immediately I make $32.12. So I'm actually making more than $15 for every MP3 player I give away. So what that does, I'm doubling my money, and I'm getting at least one and probably multiple, probably four, five subscribers to my podcast for every single one that I give away. So now I can spend $1,000, $2,000, $3,000 a day in ads profitably to build my podcast. And if you're probably watching the charts, we've been hovering in the business category number one, two, or three pretty much every single day since this has launched. Because we are able to physically drive people in. I don't know anybody else who has a podcast that can pay and be profitable to get members into it, and that's kind of the magic behind the model.

Paul Colligan:

Oh man.

Russell Brunson:

This is my gift to podcasting as we know it.

Paul Colligan:

You know it's funny, in the history of the *Podcast Report*, the most popular episode is one I did with Ed Rush where he was talking about how he essentially was buying customers for his fishing podcast. And I have a feeling this episode is going to be huge as well. You know there is these themes in podcasting, "You've got to get a fantastic mic. You need to spend at least three years of your life researching microphones, " and here is Russell doing it in his car. Then you gotta wait for people to show up because everything is free. And yes, the podcast is still free, but Russell is spending 15 bucks to get a new listener. But the cool thing is, because he is not a dumb guy, he is actually making 30 bucks to get a new listener. So he is getting new listeners and essentially doubling his money.

Russell Brunson:

And that's before they start consuming from listening to the podcast and buying our products and everything else. That's just immediately before anything else even happens, which is crazy.

Paul Colligan:

Is paying for customers the only way?

Russell Brunson:

No. The cool thing about this is that it stimulates everything else. So right now, because we are paying for these customers there is a surge of people coming in. Like now we are ranked really high in the iTunes Store. And because of that I'm watching my subscribers, now that I hooked up the analytics and stuff, we're watching our downloads are seeing this huge spike. I'd say half is from the pay stuff, but because the pay stuff is happening, it's stimulating all of the organic stuff. We are listed, we're showing up. More people are jumping in who have never heard of us. They didn't know about the MP3 player but it's happening and it's growing from that side as well. And so, I always look at it like this - we have this concept here in our office - we call it paid viral videos. Everyone wants to make a viral video that goes huge. So as good as I think I am, none of my videos go viral. But we can create something that is good enough and I could put money behind it to stimulate the growth. And then because we are putting money behind it, more people see it and then it becomes viral, and that's how we've had all of our big successes from paid viral stuff. We are stimulating it with cash. And I feel like it's the same thing here. Because we're doing this part of it, it's putting us out there and then everything else, all of the organic stuff, becomes ten times better because we are there. We are in front of people's faces now.

Paul Colligan:

There are two audiences for this show. There are those generally listening, generally interested in podcasting, that listen to everything and enjoy the show and what we do here. And I love the hobbyists, I love the enthusiasts. Welcome. The second audience for this show are the ones who become my clients - the ones that become your clients are the ones that spend real money to play this game. Because they realize that when you spend money there is actually revenue to be made for it on the other side. Now obviously, somebody doesn't start with a thousand dollars to just wait and see what happens tomorrow. You build into it. You grow into it. I think the audience that is mine, the audience, my client, your client, I think they've been spoken to. But if I am a beginning podcaster. If I am an early podcaster, should I take Russell's advice and just do this for like five years and then wake up? Or should I be a little bit more strategic? What does the, for the lack of a better term, "normal" podcaster have to learn from Russell's story?

Russell Brunson:

Yeah, so this is the biggest thing I would say, and I talk about this with my clients all of the time. Half of business or whatever it is, is you finding your voice, right? Most people want to show the highlight reel of where they are at, but they don't want to do the work to get there. And I always tell people I'm so grateful that I didn't know how to look at my stats. I had no stats on my podcast for the first year and a half. It's because I didn't stress about that and I was just doing it. And if you look at my podcast, you can go back to episode one and see, in fact the first 250 episodes are on the MP3 player. The first episode, I was not really good. Second one, I was not really good. Third, fourth... Steven here who sits behind me is telling me the first 40 or so episodes of yours, like they were good but you hadn't hit your stride yet. It was about 40 or 45 you hit your stride and you found your voice. And then like, all of a sudden it snowballs. I don't care what platform you're on. If you're podcasting, you're on Facebook Live, you're on Periscope, you're on Snapchat, whatever it is, I think the consistency of it, even if you are never planning on making money with it, it's the key to you finding your voice. If you look at videos from me, anything from three, four, five, six years ago, I wasn't polished. But I had to do it a lot, over and over and over again. You start finding your voice. What's interesting is that as you're doing things, you'll find out, like you said with your podcast, like some episodes people go crazy for and other ones they don't. It makes you think, "Why is that one interesting? Why do people care about that?

You look at it and you think, "I talked about this, that must be what they want." So you share more of that. It's just a cool organic thing where, by the consistency of you doing it, and I think at least multiple times a week, but daily if you can, the consistency of publishing something - whether it be podcast, blogging, video, something as long as you are consistently doing it. The first hundred episodes or whatever is not about your audience. The first hundred episodes is about you finding your voice. After you found your voice, at that point your audience will have found you and it'll grow and you will learn what they actually want, and you'll become better and better and better. You look at now, like I am really clear what my message is today. The reason my company is growing the way it is, is because I know what my message is. I'm completely congruent with it; everything we are doing is coming from that standpoint. But it took me, honestly twelve years to figure out what my message was, because I was publishing stuff daily, over and over and over again. As soon as you figure that out and you see what people respond to and what people resonate with, you start defining the thing that gets better and better and better and eventually you have your voice. You have your message and that is where you can start really impacting people. But you can't get to that point by you know, by just buying a nice microphone and polishing up. It comes from consistent repetition of you doing it. At that point when you've done it a hundred episodes, maybe that point, your hobby, your goal never is to make money, that's fine, just make a difference another way, like that's totally cool, but the way you are going to do that is by mastering your voice and then mastering your message. And the only way to get that is from consistent constant repetition. That's the key.

Paul Colligan:

Alright, if you want more from Russell, you can head out to iTunes. He's top of the business charts, top of the managing marketing charts. I still laugh every time I say management and marketing charts, because those are two groups that should not listen to the same podcast. iTunes if you are listening, you might want to think about that one. You can get more about Russell there. But you could also, if you head out to thepodcastreport.com/115, Russell is giving us an extended offer into this free MP3 player and you guys can pick that up. Listen to the show and definitely listen to episodes 1 through 40 and get some inspiration. I'm getting better like Russell said. But at the same time, follow through on the funnels. Take screenshots of everything. Take a look at what's happening. It's pretty fantastic. And Russell is a smart guy and a good friend and I'm thrilled to have him here on the show. So Russell, any final words?

Russell Brunson:

Two quick things, number one I want to kind of reference what you said. Buy the MP3 player and go through it slowly, not because I care about your money but because I care about you learning the process. In my group we talk about this concept called Funnel Hacking and so I want you to Funnel Hack. Look at what we are doing and why we are doing it, because if you understand that you can replicate and model it. And number two, if you like Paul, in ClickFunnel I can make what we call a Share Funnel of my podcast funnel. I can give it to you and you can give it to your audience so if anyone has a ClickFunnels account they can click the button and my entire podcast funnel will be on their account and then they can use that and edit it to make it their own. If that would be a benefit, I could give it to you and you can put that in your share notes as well.

Paul Colligan:

Oh man, let's do that! That would be really, really cool. And then we can get a link to ClickFunnels as well for those of you who don't know about it. Very cool Russell. This is a great way to kick off season four. I wanted to open the eyes of everyone to what is possible. There are other shows where you can do microphone shootouts or the hosting debates. And we are actually going to have some hosting people here in the future. But thank you for listening everyone to Season 4 Episode 1. Russell, it's always a blast to chat with you my friend.

Russell Brunson:

Appreciate it.

Paul Colligan:

And that was Russell Brunson. There is a little something in that interview for every single one of us. The links Russell spoke about are online at ThePodcastReport.com/115. I've asked Russell to keep the MP3 player offer going on as long as he can. Yes it's an affiliate link, so I want to use that.

Made in the USA
San Bernardino, CA
13 October 2018